Roman Army Units in the Eastern Provinces (1)

31 BC – AD 195

Raffaele D'Amato • Illustrated by Raffaele Ruggeri

Series editor Martin Windrow

First published in Great Britain in 2017 by Osprey Publishing

PO Box 883, Oxford, OX1 9PL, UK

1385 Broadway, 5th Floor, New York, NY 10018, USA

E-mail: info@ospreypublishing.com

Osprey Publishing, part of Bloomsbury Publishing Plc

© 2017 Osprey Publishing Ltd.

A CIP catalogue record for this book is available from the British Library

Print ISBN: 978 1 47282 176 8

PDF ebook ISBN: 978 1 47282 179 9

ePub ebook ISBN: 978 1 47282 178 2

Editor: Martin Windrow

Index by Sharon Redmayne

Typeset in Helvetica Neue and ITC New Baskerville

Map by JB Illustrations

Originated by PDQ Media, Bungay, UK

Printed in China through Worldprint Ltd

17 18 19 20 21 10 9 8 7 6 5 4 3 2 1

Osprey Publishing supports the Woodland Trust, the UK's leading woodland conservation charity. Between 2014 and 2018 our donations are being spent on their Centenary Woods project in the UK.

To find out more about our authors and books visit **www.ospreypublishing.com**. Here you will find extracts, author interviews, details of forthcoming events and the option to sign up for our newsletter.

TITLE PAGE 1st-century AD tombstone from Mainz, commemorating Maris Casitilius, a mounted archer of the *Ala Parthorum et Araborum*. It shows him with his servant carrying a bundle of javelins, confirming that such cavalrymen used a range of weapons; note also the bow-case hung from the saddle behind his leg. Also mentioned in the inscription are Maris's father Casitus, and his brother and comrade Masicates; all have Semitic names, but Tigranus, another soldier who contributed to this monument, was possibly Armenian, as was Variagnes, the commander of their auxiliary unit. (Photo courtesy Dr Stefano Izzo)

BACK COVER Helmet of Imperial Gallic type (see Plate B1); and secondary figure from monument to the tribune T. Flavius Mikkalos, both from Thracia. The figure depicts a Thracian-style helmet, and a corselet shaped low over the abdomen, so presumably of leather; note, too, the long-sleeved tunic. (Photos courtesy private collection, National Archaeological Museum, Plovdiv; and National Archaeological Museum, Istanbul)

Dedication

To all the peoples and races of the Near East, that they may remember the greatness of a common culture, and the importance of protecting the shared patrimony of all humankind.

Acknowledgements

It is my pleasant duty to acknowledge all those who helped me in this enterprise, either through assisting my access to collections, providing illustrations, helping me in my travels, or in many other ways. The available space forbids more than a bare mention of those who are in many cases dear friends and valued colleagues. I wish to record my thanks to Dr Marina Mattei, curator of the Capitolini Musei, Rome; and, as always, to Prof Livio Zerbini of Ferrara University.

In Turkey, to the General Directorate of the Turkish Ministry of Culture; the staffs of the Halûk Perk Müzesi and the Hisart Diorama Museum in Istanbul, and in particular Dr Av Halûk Perk, Dr Nejat Çuhadaroğlu, Prof Metin Gökçay, and Dr Ahmet Yavuzkır of the Sanliurfa Museum. Dr Dick Ossemann courteously shared photos taken during our common and separate travels in the country.

For the Egyptian material, to Dr Ashraf Nageh, Consultant of the Coptic Museum – Office of the General Secretary of the Supreme Council of Antiquities. While it was impossible to visit the monuments in Cyrenaica, my thanks to Luca Bonacina for his splendid photos, and to Dr David Xavier of the Roman Officer Museum permanent collection, from which important items are published here for the first time.

Regarding Romania, to Dr Radu Ciobanu, Professor in the Département des Antiquités de l'Ecole Normale Supérieure de Paris, and scientific researcher in archaeology at the National Museum of Alba Julia; to Dr Gica Baestean, Director of the Archaeological Museum of Sarmizegetusa; and to Dr Constantin Chera, Director of the Museum of Natural History and Archaeology of Constanța, who allowed me to make a careful analysis of the Ostrov helmets.

For the material from Serbia, Albania and Bulgaria, to Dr Aleksandra Sojic, Dr Stoyan Popov of Sofia, and Mr Vatev, who assisted my access to important new finds from Plovdiv.

Special photographic credit goes to Dr Stefano Izzo, whose precious archive on Roman arms and armours is always of great help, and also to the following museums and institutions: the Belgrade National Museum, National Museum of Požarevac in Serbia, National Historical Museum of Albania in Tirana, Archaeological Museum of Ancient Corinth, Archaeological Museum of Thessalonika, Skopje Archaeological Museum of Macedonia, National History Museum in Sofia, Tropaeum Traiani Museum in Adamklisi, Istanbul Archaeological Museum, Aydin Archaeological Museum, Aphrodisia Archaeological Museum, Side Archaeological Museum, Antalya Archaeological Museum, Museum of Archaeology and Ethnography in Izmit, Amasra Museum, Museum of Anatolian Civilizations in Ankara, Kayseri Archaeological Museum, Trabzon Museum, Silifke Museum, Şanlıurfa's Haleplibahçe Museum, Medusa Cam Eserler Muzesi of Gaziantep, Pierides Museum and Paphos District Archaeological Museum in Cyprus, National Museum of Archaeology of Crimea in Simferopol, Cairo Egyptian Museum, Alexandria National Museum, the British Museum, Archaeological Museum of the American University in Beirut, Israel Antiquities Authority and Prof Ronny Reich, Leptis Magna Museum, and Assaraya Alhamra Museum of Tripoli.

Finally, and as so often, my thanks for the inestimable help of my friends Dr Andrea Salimbeti and Dr Andrei Negin (I owe the latter for some superb illustrations), and for the valuable collaboration of my friend Massimo Bizzarri, my *Agens in Rebus* in the capital of the Empire. Last but not least, I am deeply grateful to Raffaele Ruggeri for his tireless and inspired work to provide magnificent new reconstructions of the soldiers of Imperial Rome. I must also acknowledge the great patience of the series editor Martin Windrow in preparing the text for publication.

Artist's Note

ROMAN ARMY UNITS IN THE EASTERN PROVINCES (1)

31 BC – AD 195

INTRODUCTION

The Eastern provinces were the rich core of the Roman Empire. Greece was the pearl of Greco–Roman civilization; Egypt was Rome's granary; and Egypt and Asia boasted opulent capitals of the Roman commonwealth such as Alexandria, Antioch and Ephesus. The desert frontiers were natural barriers against Parthia, the great oriental enemy, but the city-states of Palmyra and Hatra were hubs for the caravan trade in precious silk. It was natural for Rome to provide these Hellenized areas, always menaced by external enemies and bloody insurrections, with strong garrisons, supported by local auxiliaries and paramilitary units in the Hellenistic tradition.

The Eastern frontier was, under Trajan, the theatre of Rome's last wave of expansion, and the vulnerability of the Danubian *limes* demanded the constant presence of large numbers of troops. The Pontic region, the Caucasus and Armenia were arenas where Rome contended with the influence of Parthia and the Steppe peoples. In the East the Roman army benefited from well-established local traditions of metal-working and the production of military equipment. Long military presence in these areas, the recruitment of local manpower, the employment of irregulars, and collaboration with allied nations all influenced the introduction of weapons and accoutrements into Roman forces which became a mosaic of traditional Roman equipment, adopted local designs, and improvisations.

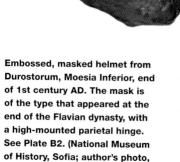

Embossed, masked helmet from Durostorum, Moesia Inferior, end of 1st century AD. The mask is of the type that appeared at the end of the Flavian dynasty, with a high-mounted parietal hinge. See Plate B2. (National Museum of History, Sofia; author's photo, courtesy of the Museum)

THE EASTERN PROVINCES

Chronology, 2nd century BC to 2nd century AD

168 BC	The Romans conquer Amphipolis, which becomes capital of Macedonia Prima.
Mid-2nd century BC	Macedonia becomes a Roman *provincia* with Thessalonika as seat of the Roman proconsul.
146 BC	Destruction of Corinth; creation of the province of Achaia.
133–129 BC	Constitution of the province of Asia.
74 BC	Cyrenaica becomes a province.
74– 67 BC	The western Pontic cities, conquered by Varro Terentius Lucullus, governor of Macedonia, are probably placed under his successors' authority.

The provinces of the Roman Empire *c.* AD 117 (plus the client Bosphoran kingdom north of the Black Sea, *Pontus Euxinus*). Under the Principate (Empire) provinces were classed as either 'Imperial' or 'senatorial'. The former were the strategic border provinces, governed by legates appointed by the Emperor and more or less heavily garrisoned with legions and auxiliary units. The senatorial provinces formed the more peaceful inner core around the Mediterranean, each governed by a proconsul appointed by the senate, with garrisons that seldom included legions. Of the provinces covered in this book, Macedonia, Achaia, Asia, Bithynia and Pontus, Cyrenaica and Creta, and Cyprus were classed as senatorial.

Note that the western limits of the provinces covered in this book are those of Dacia, Moesia, Epirus and Cyrenaica. Provinces west of these are discussed in MAA 506, *Roman Army Units in the Western Provinces (1)*. (Map by JB Illustrations)

64–62 BC	Pompey the Great creates the provinces of Asia, Bithynia, Pontus, Cilicia and Syria.
63 BC	Pompey and his army enter Jerusalem, invited in during a civil war in the Hasmonean kingdom of Israel.
43–27 BC	Constitution of the *provinciae* of Cilicia (new constitution), Lycia and Pamphilia.
30 BC	Egypt becomes *provincia Aegyptus*, ruled by an Imperial *praefectus* of equestrian rank.
27 BC	Octavian Caesar takes titles Augustus and Princeps as, in all but name, the first Emperor. Epirus is placed under the jurisdiction of the senatorial province of Achaia, except for northern part assimilated into Macedonia.
25 BC	Galatia is transformed from an allied kingdom into a province.
AD 1–15	Creation of the new province of Moesia. The territory of today's Dobruja is placed under the client Odrysian Kingdom of Thrace, but related Greek coastal cities are annexed to the Empire.
AD 6	Judaea is annexed as a province.
AD 14	Death of Augustus, succeeded by Tiberius.
AD 17	Cappadocia is transformed into a province.
AD 34–36	War with Parthia.
AD 37	Death of Tiberius, succeeded by Gaius 'Caligula'.

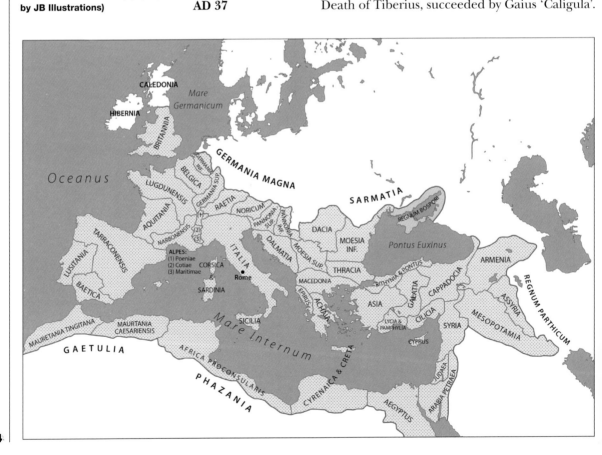

AD 41	Assassination of Caligula, succeeded by Claudius.
AD 46	On the death of King Rhoemetalces III of Thrace an anti-Roman revolt is crushed by Gallic troops. The kingdom, with the southern Thracian territories, is annexed to the Empire as the province of Thracia.
AD 47–50	Tomis (Constanţa, on the Black Sea coast of modern Romania) becomes the headquarters of the governor of Moesia.
AD 53	The Parthians invade Armenia.
AD 54	Death of Claudius, succeeded by Nero.
AD 58–63	Campaigns against the Parthians in Armenia.
AD 66	Outbreak of 'First Jewish Revolt'.
AD 67	T. Plautius Silvanus Aelianus subjugates the Sarmatian Roxolanae, Dacians and Bastarnae, and imposes Roman authority over the western coast of the Black Sea north of the lower Danube.
AD 68–69	Suicide of Nero; brief successions of Galba, Otho and Vitellius; after civil wars, during which he invades Moesia, Vespasian secures the throne.
AD 70	Siege and fall of Jerusalem. Veterans of Legio VIII Augusta settle Deultum, the only colony of free Roman citizens in Thracia.
AD 72	Campaign in Commagene.
AD 79	Death of Vespasian, succeeded by Titus.
AD 73	Fall of Masada ends First Jewish Revolt.
AD 81	Death of Titus, succeeded by Domitian.
AD 85	Dacians under Decebalus invade Moesia.
AD 86	Domitian divides *provincia Moesia* into Moesia Superior, west of Tsibrita river, with capital at Singidunum, and Moesia Inferior, with capital at Tomis.
AD 86–89	Campaigns against Dacians.
AD 96	Assassination of Domitian, succeeded by Nerva.
AD 98	Death of Nerva, succeeded by Trajan.
AD 101–102	Wholesale reorganization of Moesia Inferior; First Dacian War.
AD 103–114	Epirus becomes a separate province, under a *procurator Augusti*; it includes the northern Ionian Islands of Corfu, Lefkada, Ithaca, Cephalonia and Zakynthos.
AD 105–106	Second Dacian War; conquered, Dacia becomes a province.
AD 106	Creation of province of Arabia in north-west part of peninsula.
AD 114–117	War against Parthia; annexation of Armenia and Mesopotamia. Revolts in Judaea and Egypt.
AD 117	Death of Trajan, succeeded by Hadrian.
AD 117–138	Cappadocia, with capital at Caesarea (Kayseri), includes Colchis, Armenia Minor and most of Pontus Polemoniacus.

AD 135–136	Suppression of Bar Kochba's 'Second Revolt' in Judaea; the province is transformed into that of Syria Palaestina, with capital at Caesarea Maritima.
AD 138	Death of Hadrian, succeeded by Antoninus Pius.
AD 157–158	Campaign in Dacia.
AD 161	Death of Antoninus, succeeded by Marcus Aurelius.
AD 162–166	Campaigns against the Parthians.
AD 180	Death of Marcus Aurelius, succeeded by Commodus.
AD 192	Assassination of Commodus leads to civil wars between rival claimants.
AD 193	Nicopolis ad Istrum and Marcianopolis, previously belonging to Thracia, are incorporated into Moesia Inferior.
AD 195	During civil wars Septimius Severus invades Mesopotamia.
AD 197	Septimius Severus secures throne, and resumes campaigns in Parthia.

The frontiers of the Roman East

To stave off the constant threat from the powerful Parthian kingdom Augustus relied on diplomacy, safeguarding Roman interests by sponsoring various client kings of 'buffer' states, of whom Herod the Great of Judaea (r. 40–4 BC) is perhaps the best known. However, strong Roman forces also remained available, and the successes of Nero's general Gn. Domitius Corbulo in AD 58 and 63 allowed the installation of pliable kings in both Armenia and Parthia. The Roman Caucasus (Colchis, on and inland from the south-east Black Sea coast north of Cappadocia), and the northern Black Sea coast (Chersonesus Tauricus), were placed under the jurisdiction of Cappadocia and Moesia Inferior respectively. In southern Crimea (Taurica) the Romans exercised direct control from a base at Charax, or through the allied Bosphoran kingdom.

Helmet from the River Jordan, mid-1st century AD. Despite the damage the magnificent embossed decoration is still clear, including figures of winged Victory, chariots, trophies, and a general. Stylistically it anticipates the later Nawa helmets from Roman Syria – see page 36. (Pergamon Museum, Berlin; drawing by Dr Andrei Negin)

In Egypt, transformed into an Imperial province, troops were settled to deal with local unrest and raids from the Nubian kingdom. During the 1st century AD small posts (*praesidia*) – e.g. Didymoi, Dios, Compasi, Mons Claudianus, etc. – were built about every 30km (19 miles) along two caravan roads leading from Koptos (now Quft) on the Nile to Myos Hormos (Quseir), and to Berenike, two important harbours on the Red Sea coast.

The eastern Danube was the focus of particular attention. The Romans regarded the Danube as a natural frontier between the Empire and the *Barbaricum*, so Trajan's conquest of Dacia was a singular event – Rome's only stable conquest north of that river. In this region, especially in Moesia Inferior, Imperial policy was grounded on a sophisticated understanding of two co-existing cultures: the Dacian Getic and the Pontic Greek. While coastal fortresses preserved their own culture and institutions for longer, Roman posts along the frontier (e.g. Novae, Durostorum, Troesmis, Noviodunum, Oescus) and inside the province (Ibida, Trophaeum Traiani) provided strong centres of Roman influence.

Permanent garrisons were the most important tool for the integration of indigenous peoples, especially in relatively peaceful provinces where the soldiers maintained relations with the civil population. Around the fortress of Trophaeum Traiani a large number of settled veterans played an important role in 'Romanization', and in Tomis veterans and officials, seafarers and marines dedicated statues and monuments to the divinities of the classical Greco-Roman pantheon. As early as 140–120 BC the Via Egnatia was built across Macedonia to facilitate military access, becoming a link between West and East. Along it, for the first two centuries of the Principate, the cities of Thessalonika, Veroia, Calindoia, Philippi and Apollonia prospered under Roman rule. The cosmopolitan character of Thessalonika, which was a transport, commercial, military and administrative hub of great importance, favoured the interchange of religious beliefs, among them the cult of Mithras, a god of Iranian origin particularly worshipped among the lower ranks of the Roman army.

DISTRIBUTION OF UNITS

The Eastern territories were garrisoned by legions supported by auxiliary units; the latter might often be recruited locally for their skills in the use of particular weapons, for instance the Iturean, Hamian and Cretan

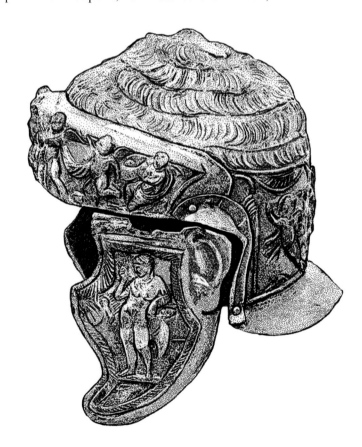

Embossed Roman cavalry helmet of Weiler typology, 1st – 2nd century AD, recovered from a grave at Pamuk Mogila, Thracia. (National Archaeological Museum, Plovdiv; drawing by Dr Andrei Negin)

archers. As in the West, the elite of the auxiliary troops were the cavalry *alae* (regiments).

(Note: For reasons of space, the reader is referred to Men-at-Arms 506, *Roman Army Units in the Western Provinces (1)*, for basic information on the recruitment, character and titling of legions and auxiliary units.)

Legiones

For the early Imperial period, from Augustus to Nero, the only legionary camps that are well known are those in Egypt. Under Augustus, Egypt was initially defended by three legions, but one was soon sent to Syria, raising that province's garrison to four legions. During the whole 1st century AD the legions were generally still a mobile force, dispatched when needed (either entire, or as detached *vexillationes*) to contribute to task forces, especially in the second half of the century. During the constitution of the province of Moesia, Legiones IIII Scytica and V Macedonica were quartered in the Timocului and Moravei valleys.

After the victories of Nero's general Corbulo the southern Black Sea port of Trapezus (Trabzond) became a major logistical base. Legio XII Fulminata ('Lightning-bolt') established its permanent camp at Melitene in Cappadocia, ready to face any invasion from the East. A frontier road linked all the legionary and auxiliary camps running from that city to the Upper Euphrates, and during the Flavian period an extensive road network also connected the Danubian legions with the Euphrates. In

Socketed and tanged arrowheads, 1st – 2nd century AD, from Nicomedia in Bithynia. Sites across the Eastern provinces have yielded countless arrowheads, in a wide variety of designs and materials. (Archaeological Museum, Izmit; author's photo, courtesy of the Museum)

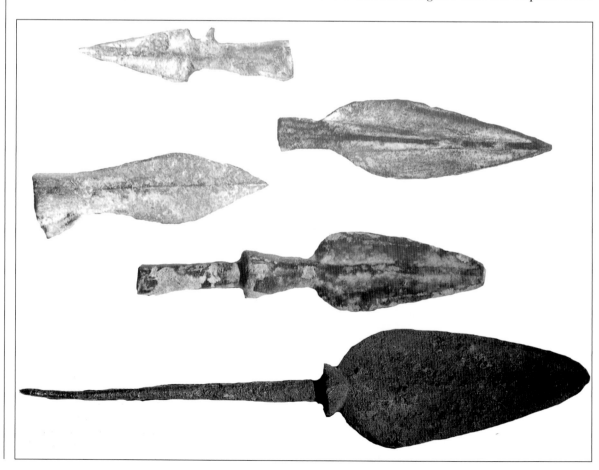

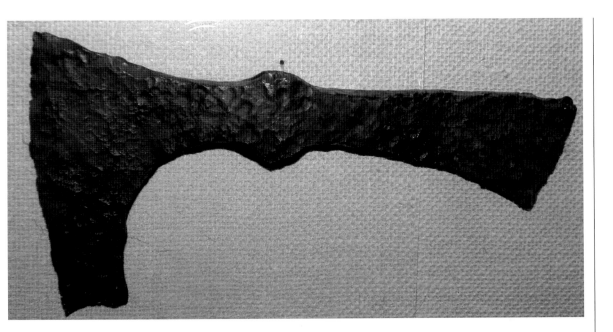

Axe-head of a legionary carpenter (*securis*) from Epirus, second half of 2nd century AD. (National Museum of Albania, Tirana; author's photo, courtesy of the Museum)

Palestine we find legionary troops at Scythopolis, Neapolis and Yoqne'am.

Although dispersed in the provinces the legions could quickly be concentrated to form field armies for major campaigns. For example, on the eve of the civil war of AD 193 the army of Pescennius Niger, stationed in Syria, mustered nine legions from Thracia, Cappadocia, Judaea, Arabia and Egypt, while the army of Severus counted 17 legions, among them those from Moesia and Dacia.

The composition of the *legio* was the same as in the Western provinces (and see page 12), but often the terms for the ranks found in sources are in Greek rather than Latin. The Roman army was called *romaikos stratos*, as attested, for example, in the inscription dedicated by the citizens of Lete to the *gymnasiarch* Manius Salarius Sabinus (AD 121). On the monument of T. Flavius Mikkalos from Perinthos (see page 22) he is called *chiliarchos legionos* (i.e. *tribunus legionis*). Many titles used in Jewish sources for Roman ranks were derived from the Greek: for example, *hegmon*, general, from the Greek *hígemón*, and *qamton*, his escort, from the Greek *comiton*. However, Latin was always the official language, and accompanied Rome's army into the East.

Auxilia

As in the Western provinces, various auxiliary units garrisoned the senatorial provinces – Achaia, Bithynia-Pontus, Cyrenaica and Macedonia – as well as the Imperial ones. When it was transformed into a province Judaea was garrisoned with six *cohortes* and one *ala*, with contingents located in Caesarea, Jerusalem, Samaria, Hebron and Ein-Gedi.

We have no references to legions being stationed in Bithynia-Pontus during the Principate, and Josephus (*BJ*, II, 366) writes that in the middle of the 1st century AD there were no military units in that province. However, from the beginning of the Empire the presence of troops there is attested in Pliny the Younger's letters, and by some military inscriptions. In the Trajanic period at least two cohorts were at the disposal of the governor, one being stationed in the capital, Nicomedia. The exact locations of other units remain undetermined, but the number of them was second only to Cyrenaica amongst senatorial provinces (seven units in Cyrenaica, five in Bithynia-Pontus and four in Asia).

Many Eastern units, unlike those stationed in the West, were billeted in or around the large cities. Tacitus termed Galatia an 'unarmed province' (*inermis provincia*), i.e. with no significant permanent Roman forces, but it was not, of course, devoid of soldiers. New excavations have shown that Gordion (ancient Vindia?) functioned, at least in part, as a military fort; auxiliaries operated in the vicinity during the second half of the 1st century AD, at about the same time that legionary bases were established along the River Euphrates at Satala and Melitene. Around AD 75–80 Galatia's provincial infrastructure underwent a major upgrade, and changes in the Anatolian military network may have required small rural posts at places that could generate supplies and protect lines of communication. Isaac correctly identified one of the most important functions of the Roman army in the East as the enforcement of political and economic control. Cilicia required a permanent garrison of no more than one auxiliary battalion, probably Cohors VI Hispanorum Equitata stationed at Tarsus in the 1st century AD.

The small Egyptian *praesidia* had garrisons of about 15 soldiers, mostly infantrymen with a few horsemen for the postal service; these were all detached from auxiliary units. Officers were low ranking, and the resident commander of a post, the *curator*, was usually only a *principalis* (senior ranker). Some of the garrisons had women with them, and satellite civilian communities provided commodities such as fresh foodstuffs, wine and female companionship. Numerous letters found at Dios show that vegetables were grown and sold at Compasi, the fort just north of Dios, where water was plentiful (a number of letters also tell us that clothes were sent there for laundering).

Numeri and *Nationes*

The Romans recruited locally for paramilitary policing duties, but on a larger scale various foreign contingents, such as those from Armenia and the Caucasus, fought in Roman armies at various dates. Josephus mentions units of oriental-style cataphract heavy cavalry, Syrian slingers and stone-throwers (*BJ*, III, 211), and Arab archers during the First Jewish Revolt (*BJ*, V, 290). At the end of the 2nd century we find the formidable Syrio-Mesopotamian *hippotoxotai* (horse-archers) sent by King Barsemios of Hatra to support Pescennius Niger against Septimius Severus, and incorporated by Niger into his army. Further *numeri* of these troops were recruited by Septimius Severus for his Parthian wars.

In addition, Rome made use of the whole armies of allied client kingdoms (*nationes*), which came with their own leaders and equipment. One example was King Antiochus of Commagene, who fought beside Titus in the siege of Jerusalem in AD 70 (*BJ*, V, 11), 'having with him a considerable number of other armed men, and a band called the Macedonian band about him, all of the same age, tall, and just past their childhood, armed and instructed after the Macedonian manner'.

Table of identified units, locations and dates

No list can pretend to be fully comprehensive. Apparent contradictions of place and date arise from, for example, fragmentary inscriptions which may indicate the presence of a detachment from a legion mainly stationed elsewhere. Sources using varying orders of words, or successive evolutions of a title, inevitably make some identifications of auxiliary units speculative. Unless specifically noted as a *cohors* or *ala milliaria* (approximately 900–1,000 strong), all auxiliary units listed here are *quingenaria* (of approximately 400–500 men) – though that word is also found explicitly included in some unit titles.

Where locations are listed, the first mention – only – gives the Roman placename, followed by (the modern placename if known), followed by the province. In subsequent mentions only the Roman placename and province are given.

Legiones:

Unit	Location	Date
Legio I Italica Antoniniana	Novae (Svishtov), Moesia Inferior	1st–3rd century
	Charax (Ai-Todor), Taurica (S. Crimea)	AD 69–108
Legio I Italica (vexillatio)	Drobetae (Drobeta-Turnu Severin), Dacia	AD 108
Legio I Adiutrix	Singidunum, Sirmium (Belgrade, Sremska Mitrovica), Moesia Superior	AD 86–92
	Dacia	AD 87–106
	Apulum (Alba Iulia), Dacia	AD 105–114
	Acumincum (Slankamen), Moesia Inferior	1st century AD
Legio I Partica	Singera (Sîngera), Dacia	2nd–3rd century AD
Legio II Augusta (vexillatio veteranorum)	Thracia	AD 77
Legio II Traiana Fortis	Samosata (Samsat), Syria	AD 114–117
Legio II Traiana (vex.)	Aelia Capitolina (Jerusalem), Judaea	AD 135–136
	Nicopolis (Alexandria), Aegyptus	2nd century AD
Legio III Augusta	Cyrenaica	AD 85–86
Legio III Augusta (vex.)	Scupi (Skopje), Moesia Superior	AD 86–88 or 90–92
Legio III Cyrenaica	Nicopolis, Aegyptus	1st century AD
Legio III Cyrenaica (vex.)	Judaea	AD 116–135
	Nova Traiana Bostra (Bosra), Syria	2nd century AD
	Arabia	2nd century AD
Legio III Gallica (vex.)	Syria	AD 66
	Judaea	AD 66–135
	Mesopotamia	AD 161
	Porolissum (Mirşid), Dacia	AD 194
	Emesa (Homs), Syria Apamene	2nd–3rd century AD
Legio III Partica	Resaina (Ras al-Ayn), Syria	2nd–3rd century AD
Legio IIII Flavia	Gornium (Kostolac), Moesia	AD 69
	Margum (Dubravica), Moesia Superior	86 – early 2nd centur AD
Legio IIII Flavia Felix (vex.)	Drobetae, Dacia	AD 105–106
	Sarmizegetusa Basileion (Gradistea Muncelului), Dacia	AD 106
	Ulpia Traiana Sarmizegetusa (Sarmigezetusa Hunedohara), Dacia	AD 108–110
	Porolissum (Pomet), Dacia	AD 106–110
	Berzobis (Berzovia), Dacia	AD 102–119
	Viminacium (Kostolac), Moesia	1st–2nd century AD
	Singidunum, Moesia Superior	2nd century AD
Legio IIII Scytica	Moesia Superior	1st century AD
Legio IIII Scytica (vex.)	Judaea	AD 66–73
	Syria	1st–2nd century AD
Legio IIII Scytica (vex.)	Doryleum (Eskisehir), Asia	2nd century AD
	Caesarea (Kayseri), Cappadocia	2nd century AD
	Antiochia (Antakya), Syria	AD 180–182
	Zeugma (Balkis), Syria	2nd–3rd century AD
Legio V Macedonica	Judaea	AD 68–73
	Moesia Inferior	1st century AD
	Troesmis (Turcoaia), Moesia Inferior	AD 106–167
Legio V Macedonica (vex.)	Doryleum, Asia	2nd century AD
	Evdokia (Tokat), Galatia	2nd century AD
	Amasea (Amasya), Cappadocia	2nd century AD
	Judaea	AD 135
	Poitassa (Turda), Dacia Porolissensis	AD 168–271
Legio VI Ferrata (vex.)	Syria	AD 66
	Judaea	AD 66
	Emesa, Syria	AD 125
	Caparcotna (Kfar Otnay), Aegyptus	AD 130
	Syria Palaestina (Judaea)	AD 135–193

Legionary organization

The internal organization of a legion differed slightly from time to time or from legion to legion, but the general picture was as follows.

Its infantry strength was c.4,800–6,200 *milites legionis*. Each of 60 *centuriae* normally had 80 men (Josephus, *BJ*, I, 15, 6), but sometimes 100, led by a *centurio* and his junior officers: the *signifer* (standard-bearer – or the *aquilifer* (eagle-bearer), in the First Century of the First Cohort); the *optio* (centurion's deputy); the *cornicen* and *bucinator* (trumpeters); and the *tesserarius* ('officer of the watchword'). A *custos armorum* was a soldier fulfilling armourer's duties; and a *beneficiarius* was a soldier or junior officer acting as a bodyguard or charged by his superior officer with other special tasks, and thus exempted from fatigue duties. The *antesignani*, a term from the Consular period meaning 'those before the standard', are still mentioned in sources of the Imperial period, as are *postsignani*, indicating picked men fighting in front of or behind the standard.

Six centuries normally formed a *cohors* (battalion) of 480–600 men (Pseudo-Hyginus, *De Mun. Castr.*, I, 7, 8, 30). The cohort might alternatively be divided into three *manipuli* each of two centuries, giving the maniple 160–200 men. Ten cohorts formed the legion (Aul. Gell., *Noct. Att.*, XVI, 4, 6); but from the Flavian period the First Cohort was of double size, with 800–1,000 men in five double-size centuries (*De Mun. Castr.*, III). This was led by the very experienced *primus pilus* ('first javelin'), the most senior of all the legion's centurions; however, in the late 1st century AD Josephus writes (*Contra Apionem*, 21, 38) that the First Cohort commander was the *tribunus laticlavius*. This young aristocrat of senatorial family was the senior of the six tribunes who assisted the legionary commander in largely administrative duties; the other five were *tribuni augusticlavii*, of the equestrian social order. The commander himself, usually of senatorial rank, was termed (like the governor of an Imperial province) the *legatus*, because he was 'delegated' by the Emperor (SHA, *Comm.*, VI, 1), and the *tribunus laticlavius* was officially this legate's second-in-command. Below the legate the senior officer with military experience was the *praefectus castrorum*, usually an ex-*primus pilus*; with responsibility for all practical aspects of the legion's duties, he took over command in the absence of the legate and senior tribune.

Each legion also had an integral cavalry unit of about 120 men, employed as scouts and couriers; they were organized in four 32-man *turmae* (squadrons), each *turma* led by a *decurio*. Each cohort of a legion also had perhaps 120 attached *calones* (servants).

For more detail, see Osprey Battle Orders 37, *The Roman Army of the Principate 27 BC–AD 117*.

Legio VI Flavia Firma	Satala (Sadak), Cappadocia	mid– AD 70
Legio VII Claudia	Charax, Taurica	AD 69
Legio VII Claudia (veterans)	Philippopolis (Plovdiv), Thracia	AD 76
Legio VII Claudia	Viminacium (Kostolac), Moesia Superior	1st–2nd century AD
	Castra Tricornia (Rytopek),Moesia Superior	2nd–3rd century AD
Legio VII Gemina Felix (vex.)	Porolissum (Pomet), Dacia	AD 194
Legio VIII Augusta	Novae, Moesia Inferior	AD 45–69
Legio VIII Augusta (vex.)	Corinth, Achaia	mid-1st cent AD
	Charax, Taurica	AD 69
	Syria	AD 69–70
Legio VIIII Hispana	Moesia	AD 86–89
	Syria	AD 131–162 ?
Legio X Fretensis	Cyrrhus (Nebi Huri), Syria	18 BC
Legio X Fretensis (vex.)	Syria	AD 66
	Judaea	AD 68–73
	Caesarea Maritima (Kesariya), Judaea	1st–2nd century AD
	Aelia Capitolina, Judaea	1st–2nd century AD
Legio XI Claudia PF	Durostorum (Silistra), Moesia Inferior	2nd century AD
	Ibida (Slava Rusă), Moesia Inferior	2nd–3rd century AD
Legio XI Ulpia Fidelis	Caesarea, Cappadocia	2nd century AD
Legio XII Fulminata	Raphanea (Rafniye), Syria	AD 66
	First Jewish Revolt	AD 66–73
	Melitene (Malatya), Cappadocia	1st–2nd century AD
Legio XII Fulminata (vex.)	Caenopolis (Vagharshapat), Cappadocia	AD 166–180
	Trapezus (Trabzon), Cappadocia	2nd century AD
Legio XIII Gemina	Apulum, Dacia	2nd century – AD 273
Legio XIII Gemina (vex.)	Nicomedia (Izmit), Bithynia	AD 197
Legio XIIII Gemina Martia Victrix	Moesia	AD 88
Legio XIIII Gemina (vex.)	Parthia (Mesopotamia)	AD 161, 198
Legio XV Apollinaris	Parthia (Mesopotamia)	AD 63–67
Legio XV Apollinaris (vex.)	Paleopaphos (Kouklia), Cyprus	AD 69
	Judaea	AD 67–73
	Heliopolis (Balbeek), Syria	AD 93 ?
	Parthia (Mesopotamia)	Trajanic period
	Caenopolis, Cappadocia	AD 166–180
	Satala, Trapezus & Pityus (Sadak, Trabzon & Pitsunda), Cappadocia	2nd century AD
Legio XVI Flavia	Sura (Suriya), Syria	2nd century AD
Legio XVI Flavia Firma	Samosata (Samsat), Syria	AD 125
Legio XVI Flavia Firma (vex.)	Karin (Erzurum), Cappadocia	2nd century AD
Legio XX Valeria Victrix (vex.)	Dacian wars	AD 103–107
Legio XXI Rapax	Moesia	AD 88
Legio XXII Deiotariana	Thebes, Nicopolis (Luxor, Alexandria), Aegyptus	1st century AD
Legio XXII Primigenia	Dacian wars	AD 101–106
	Parthian wars	AD 114–117
Legio Arabica	(?)	late 2nd century AD

Auxilia - Cohortes

Cohors Apuleia CR	Cappadocia	AD 135
Cohors Augusta	(Jerusalem), Judaea	1st century AD
Cohors Bosporiana Miliaria Sagittaria	Cappadocia	AD 135
Cohors Cypria	Sinop (Sinope), Bithynia & Pontus	1st century AD
Cohors Cyrenaica Sagittaria Equitata	Cappadocia	AD 135
Cohors Dacorum	Syria	2nd century AD
Cohors Ituraeorum eq	Cappadocia	AD 135
Cohors Miliaria	Syria	1st century AD
Cohors Scutata CR	Aegyptus	AD 143
Cohortes I-VI Commagenorum	Commagene, Syria	mid-1st century AD
Cohors I Aelia Gaesatorum mil.	Resculum (Bologa), Dacia	AD 110–161
Cohors I Antiochensium	Moesia Superior	AD 93
	Drobetae, Dacia	2nd century AD
Cohors I Apamenorum	Cappadocia	1st century AD
Cohors I Apamenorum Sagittariorum eq	Aegyptus	AD 145
Cohors I Ascalonitanorum Sagittariorum Felix eq	Syria	AD 157
Cohors I Augusta	Syria	1st–2nd century AD
Cohors I Augusta Ituraeorum Sagittaria	Dacia	AD 110–158
Cohors I Augusta Lusitanorum	Judaea	1st–2nd century AD
Cohors I Augusta Nervia Pacensis Brittonum mil	Dacia	AD 145–161
Cohors I Augusta Pannoniorum	Aegyptus	AD 83
Cohors I Augusta Praetoria Lusitanorum eq.	Aegyptus	AD 156
Cohors I Augusta Thracum	Judaea	1st–2nd century AD
Cohors I Aurelia Antonina Hemesenorum mil	Castra Micia (Vețel), Dacia	2nd century AD
Cohors I Aurelia Brittonum mil.	Porolissum, Dacia	2nd century AD
Cohors I Aurelia Dardanorum	Naissus (Nis), Moesia Superior	2nd century AD
Cohors I Batavorum mil.	Dacia	2nd century AD

Cohors I Bracaugustanorum	Moesia Inferior	AD 86–99
	Castrum Angustia (Brețcu), Dacia	2nd century AD
Cohors I Bracarum CR	Nigrinianis (Dolno Ryahovo), Moesia Inferior	AD 145
Cohors I Britannica mil. CR	Dacia	AD 106–161
Cohors I Brittonum mil. eq. Ulpia Torquata PF	Porolissum, Dacia	AD 106–191
Cohors I Bosporanorum mil.	Cappadocia	1st century AD
Cohors I Campestris	Amastri (Amasra), Bithynia & Pontus	AD 135
	Nigrinianis, Moesia Inferior	AD 145
Cohors I Claudia Sugambrorum Veterana	Nigrinianis, Moesia Inferior	AD 145
	Syria	AD 193
Cohors I Cretum Sagittariorum eq.	Gortyna (Gortina), Creta	1st century AD
	Moesia Superior	1st century AD
	Dacian wars	AD 102–105
	Egeta (Brza Palanka), Dacia	AD 160–161
Cohors I Damascena Armeniaca	Judaea	1st–2nd century AD
Cohors I Damascenorum	Judaea	AD 139
Cohors I Flavia Bessorum	Castra Tricornia (Rytopek), Moesia Superior	AD 100–120
	Macedonia	AD 120
Cohors I Flavia Chalcidenorum Sagittariorum eq.	Syria	AD 157
Cohors I Flavia Cilicum eq.	Aegyptus	AD 140
Cohors I Flavia CR eq.	Judaea	2nd century AD
Cohors I Flavia Commagenorum	Dacia	AD 157
Cohors I Flavia Hispanorum mil. eq. PF	Moesia	1st century AD
	Dacian wars	AD 101–106
Cohors I Flavia Ulpia Hispaniorum eq. CR	Moesia Superior	from AD 94
Cohors I Flavia Numidarum	Lycia	AD 161–162
	Dacia	AD 110–161
Cohors I Gallorum	Nigrinianis, Moesia Inferior	AD 145
Cohors I Gallorum Dacica	Dacia	AD 157
Cohors I Germanorum mil. Eq.	Cappadocia	AD 135
Cohors I Germanorum CR	Nigrinianis, Moesia Inferior	AD 145
Cohors I Hispanorum	Dacia	2nd century AD
Cohors I Hispanorum eq.	Cappadocia	early Principate
	Cyrenaica	early Principate
	Aegyptus	early Principate – late 1st century AD
	Judaea-Arabia	2nd century AD
Cohors I Hispanorum Veterana eq.	Stobi (Gradsko), Macedonia	early Principate
	Moesia Inferior	AD 99
	Brectu (Buridava), Dacia Inferior	AD 121
	Dacia Porolissensis	AD 145–161
Cohors I Ituraeorum	Dacia	2nd century AD
Cohors I Lepidiana eq. CR	Moesia Inferior	AD 98–114
Cohors I Lucensium eq.	Syria	2nd century AD
Cohors I Lusinatorum Cyrenaica eq.	Nigrinianis, Moesia Inferior	AD 145
Cohors I mil. Sagittariorum	Masada, Judaea	AD 73 – 2nd century AD
Cohors I Montanorum	Dacia	2nd century AD
	Judaea	AD 139
Cohors I Numidarum mil. eq. Sagittaria	Cappadocia	AD 135
	Lycia-Pamphylia	AD 178
Cohors I Raetorum eq.	Cappadocia	AD 135
Cohors I Sagittariorum mil. eq.	Tibiscum (Jupa), Dacia	2nd century AD
Cohors I Sebastenorum mil.	Judaea	AD 139
Cohors I Silicum Sagittariorum	Nigrinianis, Moesia Inferior	AD 145
Cohors I Sugambrorum Veterana eq.	Moesia	AD 26–77
	Moesia Inferior	AD 91–145
	Syria	AD 157
Cohors I Tebaeorum eq.	Aegyptus	AD 114
Cohors I Thracum mil.	Judaea	AD 86–90
	Ein-Gedi, Judaea	AD 124–128
	Tiberias (Hebron), Judaea	AD 128–186
Cohors I Thracum Syriaca	Timacum Minus, Moesia Superior	1st–2nd century AD
	Judaea	2nd century AD
	Nigrinianis, Moesia Inferior	AD 145– 157
Cohors I Thracum Sagittariorum	Timacum Minus (Ravna),Moesia Superior	1st–2nd century AD
	Judaea	2nd century AD
	Nigrinianis, Moesia Inferior	AD 145– 157
Cohors I Thracum Sagittariorum	Dacia	AD 157– 158
Cohors I Tyiriorum	Moesia Inferior	1st century AD
Cohors I Ubiorum	Moesia Inferior	1st century AD
	Dacia	AD 157
Cohors I Ulpia Afrorum eq.	Aegyptus	AD 177
Cohors I Ulpia Brittonum mil.	Bologa, Dacia	early 1st cent AD
	Porolissum, Dacia	AD 106 – mid-3rd cent
Cohors I Ulpia Dacorum	Cappadocia	AD 135
	Syria	AD 157
Cohors I Ulpia Galatarum	Judaea	AD 139
Cohors I Ulpia Petraeorum mil. eq.	Syria	2nd century AD
Cohors I Ulpia Sagittariorum eq.	Syria	2nd century AD
Cohors I Ulpia Sagittariorum eq.	Syria	2nd century AD

Cavalry *spatha* from North Africa, late 1st– early 2nd century AD. This bronze-furnished iron sword comes from an old English private collection; the pommel and grip are made of ivory, both with elaborate engraving. (David Xavier Collection; author's photo)

Cohors I Vindelicorum mil.	Dacia	AD 157
Cohors II Aurelia Dacorum	Porolissum, Dacia	2nd century AD
Cohors II Aurelia Dardanorum	Moesia Superior	2nd century AD
Cohors II Bracaraugustanorum et classicorum	Nigrinianis, Moesia Inferior	AD 145
Cohors II Britannica	Porolissum, Dacia	AD 106 – mid-3rd cent
Cohors II Brittonum Flavia eq.	Moesia Inferior	AD 99
Cohors II Brittonum mil. CR PF	Moesia	AD 103
	Dacia	2nd century AD
Cohors II Cantabrorum	Judaea	1st–2nd century AD
Cohors II Chalcidenorum	Moesia Inferior	1st century AD
Cohors II Classica Sagittaria	Syria	AD 157
Cohors II Equitum	Syria	2nd century AD
Cohors II Flavia Bessorum	Moesia Inferior	1st century AD
	Dacia	AD 129
Cohors II Flavia Brittonum	Nigrinianis, Moesia Inferior	AD 145
Cohors II Flavia Commagenorum eq. Sagittariorum	Commagene, Syria	AD 60
	Moesia Superior	AD 95–99
	Moesia Inferior	AD 100
	Dacian wars	AD 102–105
	Castra Micia, Dacia	AD 105–249
Cohors II Flavia Numidarum	Dacia	AD 129
Cohors II Gallorum et Ubiorum	Moesia Inferior	AD 99
Cohors II Gallorum Macedonica eq.	Moesia Superior	1st century AD
Cohors II Hispanorum	Resculum, Dacia	AD 110–115
Cohors II Hispanorum eq .	Galatia	1st century AD
	Aegyptus	AD 134
	Cappadocia	AD 135
	Syria	2nd century AD
Cohors II Hispanorum Scutata Cyrenaica eq.	Cyrenae, Cyrenaica	mid-1st century AD
	Moesia Superior	2nd century AD
	Dacia	AD 145–161
Cohors II Italica CR	Jerusalem, Judaea	1st century AD
Cohors II Italica CR Sagittariorum mil. Eq.	Cappadocia	AD 135
Cohors II Lucensium	Moesia Inferior	1st century AD
Cohors II Lusitanorum eq.	Aegyptus	2nd century AD
Cohors II Mattiacorum	Nigrinianis, Moesia Inferior	AD 145
Cohors II Thracum	Judaea	1st–2nd century AD
Cohors II Thracum eq.	Egypt	AD 167
Cohors II Thracum Syriaca eq.	Syria	AD 157
Cohors II Ulpia eq. CR	Syria	AD 157
Cohors II Ulpia Galatarum	Judaea	AD 139
Cohors II Ulpia Paflagonum eq.	Syria	2nd century AD
Cohors III Augusta Cyrenaica	Cappadocia	AD 135
Cohors III Augusta Thracum eq.	Syria	AD 157
Cohors III Bracarum	Judaea	AD 139
Cohors III Brittonum	Moesia Superior	AD 103
	Dacia	2nd century AD
Cohors III Callaecorum Bracaraugustanorum	Judaea	AD 87–139
Cohors III Campestris	Cuppae (Golubag), Moesia Superior	2nd century AD
Cohors III Campestris CR	Drobetae, Dacia	AD 110
	Moesia Superior	AD 160-161
Cohors III Coll (?)	Syria	1st century AD
Cohors III Commagenorum	Dacia	2nd century AD
Cohors III Cypria CR	Philippopolis (Plovdiv), Thracia	after AD 103
Cohors III Dacorum	Porolissum, Dacia	AD 194
Cohors III Dacorum eq.	Syria	2nd century AD
Cohors III Gallorum	Dacia	AD 129
Cohors III Ituraeorum	Aegyptus	AD 103
Cohors III Thracum Syriaca eq.	Syria	2nd century AD
Cohors III Ulpia Galatarum	Judaea	AD 139
Cohors III Ulpia Paflagonum eq.	Syria	2nd century AD
Cohors III Ulpia Petraeorum mil. eq. Sagittaria	Arabia	AD 107
Cohors IIII Hispanorum eq.	Dacia Superior	AD 158
Cohors IIII Lucensium eq.	Syria	2nd century AD
Cohors IIII Raetorum	Moesia Superior	AD 93–103
Cohors IIII Raetorum eq.	Lycia-Pamphylia	AD 114
	Cappadocia	AD 135
Cohors IIII Thracum Syriaca eq.	Syria	AD 157
Cohors IIII Ulpia Petraeorum	Judaea	AD 139
Cohors V Chalcidenorum eq.	Syria	2nd century AD
Cohors V Gallorum	Transdierna (Tekija), Moesia Superior	1st–2nd century AD
Cohors V Gemina CR	Judaea	AD 139
Cohors V Hispanorum eq.	Moesia Superior	2nd century AD
Cohors V Lingonum	Porolissum, Dacia	AD 106–215
Cohors V Ulpia Petraeorum mil. eq.	Syria	2nd century AD
Cohors VI Breucorum	Viminacium, Moesia Superior	1st century AD
Cohors VI Equestris	Bithynia	2nd century AD
Cohors VI Hispanorum eq.	Tarsus, Cilicia	1st–2nd century AD
Cohors VI Thracum	Porolissum, Dacia	AD 106 – mid-3rd cent
Cohors VI Ulpia Petraeorum	Judaea	AD 139
Cohors VII Breucorum eq.	Vindia (Gordion ?), Galatia	1st–2nd century AD
	Cyprus	AD 115–116

Cohors VII Gallorum	Moesia Inferior	1st–2nd century AD
	Syria	AD 132–157
Cohors VII Campestris	Syria	2nd century AD
Cohors VII Ituraeorum	Aegyptus	1st century AD
Cohors VIII Raetorum CR	Dacia	AD 106–110
Cohors IX (VIIII) Gemina,	Transdierna, Moesia Superior	1st–3rd century AD
Voluntariorum		
Cohors XIII Hispanorum	Macedonia	1st century AD
Cohors XX Palmyrenorum eq.	Dura Europos, Mesopotamia	2nd–3rd century AD

Alae:

Ala Antoniniana Gallorum	Judaea	AD 139
Ala Apriana	Tebe-Syene-Saqqara, Aegyptus	1st– 2nd cents AD
Ala Atectorigiana	Moesia Inferior	1st century AD
Ala Augusta	Aegyptus	1st century AD
Ala Augusta	Augusta (Hărlec), Moesia Inf.	1st century AD
Ala Augusta Germaniciana	Cappadocia	1st century AD
Ala Augusta Syriaca	Syria	1st–2nd century AD
Ala Bosporanorum	Syria	1st century AD
	Dacia	2nd century AD
Ala Claudia Nova	Moesia Inferior	2nd century AD
Ala Commagenorum	Commagene, Syria	AD 17/18
Ala Gallorum et Thracum	Judaea	AD 139
Ala Gallorum Veterana	Aegyptus	AD 199
Ala Gaetulorum Veterana	Judaea	AD 66–73
Ala Milliaria	Dacia	2nd century AD
Ala Pia Gemina Sebastena	Samaria, Judaea	1st century AD
Ala Sebastenorum	Caesarea, Judaea	1st century AD
Ala Thracum Herculiana mil.	Syria	AD 136– 157
Ala Veterana Gaetolorum	Judaea	1st–2nd century AD
Ala Vocontiorum	Koptos, Aegyptus	AD 134
Ala I Asturum	Moesia Inferior	AD 99
Ala I Augusta Eracarum	Dacia Inferior	AD 140
Ala I Augusta Gemina Colonorum	Cappadocia	1st–2nd century AD
Ala I Batavorum mil.	Apulum (Critesti), Dacia Porolissensis	AD 158
Ala I Bosporanorum	Syria	1st century AD
	Dacia	2nd century AD
Ala I Bracaraugustanorum	Moesia Inferior	AD 99
Ala I Claudia Gallorum	Moesia Inferior	AD 99–105
	Dacia	2nd century AD
Ala I Commagenorum	Aegyptus	1st century AD
Ala I Flavia Gaetulorum	Moesia Inferior	2nd century AD
Ala I Gallorum Atectorigiana	Nigrinianis, Moesia Inferior	AD 145
Ala I Gallorum Flaviana	Nigrinianis, Moesia Inferior	AD 145
Ala I Gallorum et Bosporanorum	Micia, Dacia	AD 107–158
Ala I Gallorum et Pannoniorum	Nigrinianis, Moesia Inferior	AD 145
	Dacia	AD 145–161
Ala I Gallorum Veterana	Aegyptus	2nd century AD
Ala I Hispanorum	Dacia	AD 129
Ala I Hispanorum Campagonum	Dacia	AD 157–158
Ala I Illyricorum	Dacia	2nd century AD
Ala I Praetoria CR	Syria	2nd century AD
Ala I Tracum Herculana	Galatia	AD 94
Ala I Thracum Mauretana	Judaea	1st–2nd century AD
	Aegyptus	AD 154–156
Ala I Tungrorum Frontoniana	Dacia	AD 118/133–245
Ala I Ulpia Dacorum	Cappadocia	AD 135
Ala I Ulpia Dromedariorum	Palmyra, Syria	AD 156/157
Palmyrenorum mil.		
	Arabia	AD 161
Ala I Ulpia Singularium	Syria	AD 157
Ala I Vespasiana Dardanorum	Nigrinianis, Moesia Inferior	AD 145
Ala II Bracaraugustanorum	Thracia	AD 114
Ala II Flavia Agrippiana	Syria	1st–2nd century AD
Ala II Gallorum	Cappadocia	AD 135
Ala II Hispanorum Aravacorum	Nigrinianis, Moesia Inferior	AD 99–145
Ala II Pannoniorum	Dacian wars	early 2nd cent AD
Ala II Pannoniorum Siliana CR	Dacia	AD 144
Torquata		
Ala II Ulpia Afrorum	Aegyptus	2nd century AD
Ala II Ulpia Auriana	Cappadocia	AD 135
Ala III Thracum	Syria	2nd century AD
Ala IIII Bracaraugustanorum	Syria	AD 88
Ala V Gallorum	Aegyptus	2nd century AD
Ala VII Phrygum	Syria	AD 131–136
	Judaea	AD 139

Numeri:

Numerus Burgariorum et	Dacia	AD 138
Veredariorum		
Numerus Palmyrenorum	Porolissum, Dacia	AD 106 – mid-3rd century
Sagittariorum		
Numerus Palmyrenorum	Tibiscum, Dacia	2nd century AD
Tibiscensium		
Numerus Pedites Singulares	Dacia	AD 110–157
Britannici		
Vexillatio Equitum Illyricorum	Dacia	AD 129

Ring-pommel sword, last quarter of 2nd century AD, found at Gaziantep, Syria. (Glass Museum, Gaziantep; author's photo, courtesy of the Museum)

ARMS, EQUIPMENT & CLOTHING

The Roman soldiers initially sent to the Eastern frontiers were equipped according to their military traditions, but over time local factors, and the semi-continuous state of war with Parthia, led to a regional diversity showing strong Hellenistic, Iranian and Mediterranean influences. These reflected climatic conditions, availability of materials, and the interchange of styles through contacts with local populations and foreign forces. The general impression given by some recovered artefacts, especially in Judaea, also emphasizes a reliance on repaired and re-used equipment over extended periods.

THE PROVINCES:

MOESIA SUPERIOR

Legionaries (predominantly from Legiones VII Claudia and IIII Flavia) left numerous traces at the camp near Viminacium. Graves are most often identified as military on the basis of belts, *fibulae* brooches, etc; weapons are uncommon, but finds do include spear- and arrowheads. The latter are normally treated as grave goods unless found within the human remains – for example, bones in Grave G-152 from Pirivoj show two arrow-wounds and one sword-cut. The deceased was judged to be a soldier based on stress marks on the bones typical for prolonged wearing of armour. Spears (Graves G1-263, G1-70) are the next most common finds, followed by swords and shields.

Grave G-24275 yielded a unique example of a body lying beneath a shield, on his back with his legs bent at the knees; the total length of the burial was 1.3m (4.26ft), and the shield covered it from head to knees. There was no trace of an *umbo* (boss), only the nailed-on iron edging being preserved. The height of the shield is 101cm (39.76ins), the width in the middle 55cm (21.65ins), the upper width 49cm (19.3ins) and the lower width 42cm (16.53 inches). Its curvature also differs between the upper and lower sections, from 19cm to 10cm deep respectively (7.5–3.9 ins). The iron binding, which preserved tiny wooden fragments, consists of straps 1.8cm (0.7in) wide and 2–3mm thick, with nails every 10–15cm (3.9–5.9 ins). As to dating, a similar burial of an auxiliary found near Serdica suggests the Antonine period.

Among finds from the auxiliary camp of Transdierna (Tekija), bronze clasps, a buckle and tie-loops from two examples of the iron *lorica segmentata* confirm that this laminated armour was not exclusive to the legions. Harness and/or belt fittings include an interesting pendant (10.8cm, 4.2ins) datable to the turn of the 1st /2nd centuries AD, with

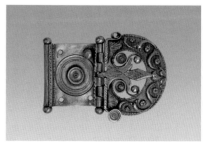

Parts of a silvered and tinned *cingulum* belt and 'apron' straps from the auxiliary fort of Transdierna (Tekija), Moesia Superior, last quarter of 1st century AD. (National Museum, Belgrade; photos courtesy Dr Aleksandra Sojic)

parallels to finds at Vindonissa. Other harness fittings have been dated to the 40s–80s AD. Bronze shield fragments (of a circular *umbo*, edging, and bronze sheet) do not allow identification of the type of shield.[1]

The Tekija site also revealed numbers of weapons all dated to the 1st–2nd centuries: four fighting knives of three distinct typologies, two of them known from other Roman sites; six spearheads and two butt ferules; and a large part of a composite bow of Trajanic date (similar to finds at Cuprija-Horreum Margi and Kostol-Pontes in the same province). Spearheads of two categories are well represented, distinguished by the relationship between the points and the shoulders; scholars have associated the narrower blades with thrown weapons and the broader with stabbing-spears. A *pelta*-shaped bronze scabbard chape can be dated between AD 157 and 211 (parallels in Stockstadt-am-Main). A bronze hilt fragment (with parallels from Pompeii) is pertinent to an auxiliary sword, and part of a bronze scabbard for a dagger of Eastern origin has parallels from Judaea. However, the most precious find from Tekija is the complete set of silvered belt fittings for a *cingulum* furnished with 'apron' straps, dated to the end of the 1st century AD. Recalling those of the famous Herculaneum belt, they were probably from an Italic workshop.

MOESIA INFERIOR

An unusual helmet from Ostrov, of Phrygian shape but with noteworthy Sarmatian influences, has an eagle-shaped *protome* which links it directly with the Jupiter cult, while two snakes, passing forward from a Medusa head at the back of the skull to meet on the front, recall the cult of Mars. This helmet may have been employed during the Hippika Gymnasia cavalry 'sports', but various images show similar helmets also being worn on the battlefield. Although dated to the late 2nd century AD, this specimen supports the hypothesis of a Thracian origin for Roman face-mask helmets, offered by Drexel and later supported by Venedikov, who pointed to some anthropomorphic cheek-pieces of Phrygian-type helmets from Thrace as obvious prototypes of the mask. (See also under 'Thracia', below.)

The monument of Adamklisi, celebrating the Roman victory over the Dacians and their Germanic and Sarmatian allies in the so-called 'Moesian Diversion' of the Dacian wars, represents an unusual use of the *pilum* javelin in hand-to-hand combat against unarmoured enemies. The Roman extra-heavy armoured legionaries, brandishing it in a phalanx formation while carrying semi-cylindrical *scuta*, wear a helmet of segmented appearance (though perhaps with cruciform reinforcing

---

1   In this text we use the adjectives bronze, brass, copper-alloy and yellow-metal generically, without pretending to distinguish scientifically between different alloys of copper with other metals.

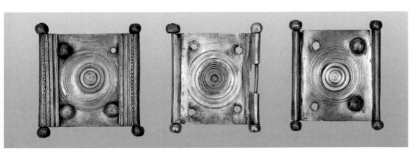

Partially masked helmet of the *'Mater Castrorum'* type, 2nd – 3rd century AD, from Durostorum in Moesia Inferior. (Constanţa Archaeological Museum; author's photo, courtesy of the Museum)

bars?), a scale cuirass worn above *pteryges*, and a *manica* laminated protector on the right arm. This *manica*, worn by at least 16 legionaries and *signiferi* standard-bearers on the monument, is of particular interest. Derived from that worn by gladiators, it was used during the Dacian wars to protect the exposed weapon-arm from the terrible blows of the enemy's scythe-like *falces*. Three *auxilia* on the monument are all armed with *spathae* with the scabbard worn on the left side of the body, as mentioned by Josephus in his description of Roman infantry. All the soldiers are wearing *caligae* sandals.

Archaeological digs in the legionary base at Novae have yielded important new evidence regarding the *lorica segmentata*. Bronze fragments correctly identified as parts of this type of armour were initially supposed by other scholars to be pieces of a *manica*, but the later find of characteristic bronze fittings fixed to pieces of bronze plate – as opposed to the usual iron – is significant. Analysis of the context of Pit Cz in Room 13, which yielded the largest number of *lorica* fragments, also proposes a change of dating. Against the thesis that the material was deposited after the arrival of Legio I Italica, Prof Sarnowski and Dr Modzelewski have dated the pit (on the basis of animal bones, pottery, and coins of Vespasian) to the last years of Legio VIII Augusta's presence at Novae, i.e. in the AD 60s, earlier than the construction of the headquarters buildings of I Italica. The pit contained four examples of the vulnerable and thus often-replaced fittings of the *lorica segmentata* of Corbridge A and B types. These come from at least two cuirasses, at least one made of bronze and another of iron; one fragment resembles others found in the *scamnum tribunorum* at Novae, where again parts of both iron and bronze armours were found. According to Gentscheva, the pieces of dark bronze sheet were pertinent to the shoulder-pieces and breast plates of armour of Corbridge A type. The rarity of such finds might suggest that this kind of armour (reconstructed in Plate B1) may have been reserved for centurions or for selected legionaries only. Other fragments of such armour were found at Oescus in the same province.

DACIA

The equipment found in Dacia must be distinguished between that worn during the conquest in the first years of the 2nd century AD, which is well depicted on monuments, and that worn by soldiers quartered there subsequently.

The civil site of Ulpia Trajana Sarmizegetusa has revealed a large quantity of military equipment, either contemporary with or successive to the Dacian wars. Two intact iron specimens of *manica* have been found on the site, one of them among battle-debris, and fragments of a third are preserved in the local museum, together with bronze shoulder-clasps from the *lorica segmentata*. Two decorations from military belts are dated to the post-conquest period (both having parallels in Germania and Pannonia).

A helmet from Berzobis (Berzovia), dated to no earlier than AD 85, is one of the first known specimens with crossed iron reinforcing bars over the skull, possibly adopted to protect against *falces* and long slashing-swords.

Some time around the turn of the 1st – 2nd centuries such braces were riveted onto the bowl of the legionary helmet, as well depicted on Trajan's Column. The archaeology shows that they were fitted retrospectively, and their crudeness suggests that they might have been added while on campaign. The exact date is unknown, but some authors ascribe their first appearance to Domitian's war against Decebalus in AD 85–89. This was not, of course, a general modification made to all Imperial Gallic or Italic helmets; the various legions adapted to the conditions they encountered.

The rich post-conquest finds of military equipment from Tibiscum include knifeblades similar to specimens from Moesia Superior (Viminacium and Tekjia) and Judaea, attesting to their employment by Eastern units stationed there. The sheath of a Roman *pugio* military dagger found at Ocnita was the most eastern find of the type until the discovery of a similar sheath from Chersonesus.

Dacia is one of the many places where local practice effected Roman equipment. The scythe-like *falx* survived in Roman use for centuries in the Eastern Empire, and the Roman army had adopted the *draco* standard, with a bronze head and a silk body, at least by the second half of the 2nd century AD.

Head of an Eastern auxiliary archer, perhaps of a *Cohors Hemesorum*, of the First Dacian War; compare with Plate F2. (Scene L, Trajan's Column, Rome, cast from Museo della civiltà Romana; author's photo, courtesy of the Museum)

MACEDONIA

Monuments give the image of a still strongly Hellenized army, with 'muscled' corselets worn over *subarmales* (under-armour jerkins) fitted with hanging strap-like *pteryges* (e.g. statue from Prilep, Skopje Museum), and round *clipei* shields. Such equipment was certainly worn by locally raised garrisons, but a certain Greek taste must also have influenced the appearance of Roman regular troops quartered there, especially cavalry and officers. The dress of warriors and soldiers on monuments and funerary *stelae* includes the short military *sagum* and longer *chlamys* cloaks, and Greek *chitones* tunics beside typical Roman equivalents.[2] Various Greek boots (*cothurni*) are depicted instead of *caligae* sandals or *calcei* closed shoes; they usually show an upper frontal tongue falling forward over the instep.

Actual Roman weapons of this period are scarce and still mainly unpublished. However, the valley of the River Vardar has yielded a gilded and inscribed hemispherical 2nd-century cavalry shield boss, together with cavalry harness fittings from c. AD 125–150.

Gilded cavalry shield *umbo* with large flat-headed rivets and punched inscription, mid-2nd century AD, from the Vardar river valley in either Moesia Superior or Macedonia. (National Museum, Skopje; author's photo, courtesy of the Museum)

EPIRUS & ACHAIA

A carpenter's axe and other camp tools, today in the Tirana Archaeological Museum, attest that this tool, often employed as a weapon by the marines, had entered the Roman army's arsenal during the 1st century AD, especially in the Eastern provinces. Generally, however, analysis of military accoutrements must rely upon the iconography. The wonderfully detailed *stele* of Gaius Valerius Valens from Corinth (reconstructed as Plate C3) shows the typical undress uniform of *tunica militaris* and

---

2   In this text the terms *stele/stelae*, gravestone/s and tombstone/s are used interchangeably to mean any kind of individual funerary monument.

The funerary altar of the actor Marcus Varinius Areskon, AD 175–200, from Thessalonika, Macedonia. He is depicted with a mask of Tragedy and in the uniform of a cavalryman, possibly indicating a role he played. The sword baldric to his left hip retains traces of red paint; the linen armour has a *pectoraris* ornamented with a geometrical pattern; and the two visible ranges of white *pteryges* were decorated with red and black lines. (Thessalonika Archaeological Museum; author's photo, courtesy of the Museum)

paenula. His *gladius* of Pompeii type is proudly displayed, as well as a *fustis* or cudgel and a stack of writing tablets.

The garments worn by the centurion Timokles on his tombstone in Epidauros are an officer's *paludamentum/chlamys* pinned at his left shoulder by a round *fibula*, short *femoralia* breeches, and high *cothurni* boots. His impressive 'muscled' armour recalls the bronze corselet described in the time of Antoninus Pius – though as rare, and reserved for senior ranks – by Pausanias (*Per.*, X, 27, 2). This armour was called a *thorax stadios* or *statos*, because, when placed upon the ground on its lower edges, it stood upright. It consisted principally of a pair of breast and back plates shaped to the torso, made of bronze, iron, or occasionally more precious metals.

Unlike those on the many statues of generals surviving in this province, the centurion's corselet shows little ornamentation, though it does feature the *zona militaris* or 'Hercules' knot', a cloth sash tied in front of the torso as a symbol of rank. His armour is worn over a *subarmalis* fitted with *pteryges*, probably made of leather faced with linen and fringed at the ends. Such armours could be fastened by two hinges on the sides and through shoulder-guards, as seen in a few surviving fragments and on many statues; others in this province show them fastened by means of buckles on both sides. If they are decorated with embossing, or with riveted and soldered appliqués, the main motif on the upper breast is usually a Gorgon's head. Metallic *pteryges* are rarely represented (e.g. on the Kythnos *loricatus*), and are part of the armour's lower border (*cymation*), under which can be seen the hanging pieces of the *subarmalis*.

The defensive equipment of Roman soldiers stationed in the Greek provinces was described by Apuleius (*Metamorphosis*, X,1): 'I was carrying his helmet... which gleamed in splendour; his shield [*scutum*], which cast its flashes far and wide on everything it passed…'.

The Antonine-period stele of Artemidoros (AD 160–180) from Athens shows the soldier dressed in a light sleeveless *colobium*, and hunting with a 'winged' spear (parallels in Thracia and Moesia Superior).

THRACIA

Thracia's wealth of military equipment finds is unparalleled in the Balkans. The richness of Thracian graves in what are today Bulgaria, Turkey and Greece attests both to the high degree of integration of Thracians in the Roman army, and to the splendid equipment of the local elite. Possible support for the theory of a Thracian origin for Roman face-mask helmets is provided by finds of several such helmets in early Thracian burials. A particularly rich mid-1st century AD grave at Vize included a masked helmet of silvered bronze, with an embossed Attic fronton (frontal band) on the bowl, embossed wavy hair, and a prominent *corona civica* of oakleaves and acorns.

The armour from Vize is a hybrid, made of ringmail incorporating small bronze and silver-plated iron scales of ridged shape (*plumata*); the mail itself is composed of alternating rows of riveted and solid rings. As in the Greek *linothorax*, the shoulders are protected by 18cm-wide (7in)

humeralia doublings extending over them from the back. The upper part of the chest is protected by a squared strip with two pairs of buttons for attaching hook fastenings for the shoulder-pieces, made of silver-plated bronze. The integrated scales were arranged to create a diamond pattern on the shoulder-doublings and hem. This armour is one of few Roman specimens in which fragments of textile lining (originally painted purple) are preserved.

Other examples of mask helmets, fitted with shallow pseudo-Attic frontons, came from the Roshava Dragana barrow at Chatalka, where the full equipment of a Romano-Thracian armoured cavalryman was found, including possible horse armour. Graves around Philippopolis (Plovdiv) have provided further prizes, like the splendid helmet of Weiler typology from Pamuk Mogila (see page 7). A unique specimen of a *gladius hispaniensis* of Mainz typology (Haltern-Camulodunum variant), but with a scabbard chape of Pompeii type and the bronze throat decorated with the Lupa Capitolina, has been found in Rajkova Mogila and dated to the turn of the 1st – 2nd centuries AD. A recent display in the Plovdiv Museum includes a new mask-helmet of 'Alexander' typology, and an unusual Weisenau-type legionary helmet (H.R. Robinson's Imperial Gallic classification – see Plate B1 and page 46).

Space prevents a listing of Thracian battlefield finds, but they include iron and bronze arrowheads, sling bullets, spear and javelin heads; a single-edged Thracian sword, short triangular daggers, and a 2nd-century *pugio* in a richly decorated scabbard; bronze *umbos* resembling the Vardar valley specimen, and iron bosses of Thracian shape. Other finds include belt furniture, a wide range of bronze and silvered harness fittings, and even torques and bracelets; camp tools (hammers, axes, *dolabrae* pickaxes); fragments of trumpets; and, from Plotinoupolis, a splendid golden military *imago* of Septimius Severus.

On the gravestone of the Flavian-period tribune Flavius Mikkalos, from Perinthos, figures are represented in Roman equipment showing

strong Greek influences. Apart from one belonging to the Italic tradition (Buggenum-Montefortino), all the helmets represented follow Hellenistic styles, being a mixture of pseudo-Attic, Boeotian and Thracian. Mikkalos's cavalry *spatha* (Tac., *Ann.*, XII, 35) is fastened on his right side. The only armour worn on the relief is the *thorax statos*, which suggested to Kramer that the other soldiers represented are centurions or junior officers. These armours are of three different typologies. One is shaped low over the abdomen (which Kramer interpreted as intended to represent leather); two others are the typical half-thorax of the late Consular and Hellenistic periods; and the apparently metal muscled cuirass of Mikkalos himself is longer, and undecorated except for the sash knotted on the breast.

Other sculptures in Thracia showing soldiers on horseback, although very simple, offer information on the tunics, cloaks, shoes, spears or javelins of local Roman provincial cavalrymen.

CYRENAICA & CRETA

Unfortunately, the armed anarchy prevailing in Libya prevented the present author from reaching its museums, but figurative monuments are rich. In Cyrenaica, the legionaries of Septimius Severus on the monuments at Leptis Magna wear pseudo-Attic helmets, sometimes embossed with animal heads on the skull and fitted with a fronton; Director Chiarucci of the Legio II Parthica Museum in Albano Laziale considers it to be an iron helmet of Hellenic influence. On the sculpted crown are visible remains of a metallic support for the plume, as well as the clasps of cheek-guards wide enough to cover the whole face – all details strongly arguing that the sculptor was copying from actual specimens. The armours depicted are Hellenistic, with muscled *loricae* worn by commanders, and legionaries, cavalrymen and Imperial bodyguards wearing laminated, scale and ringmail armours. A *praepositum militum* is depicted clad in *tunica* and *sagum* and holding a *vitis* rank-baton and a staff.

Depictions of officers and soldiers show the late 2nd-century Severan transition of costumes from the previous Antonine period: they now wear combinations of long-sleeved tunic, cloak (*sagum* or *paenula*), long or short trousers, and closed shoes (*calcei*). The *praepositum militum* has a ring-buckled belt, as became typical in the 3rd century. The reliefs at Leptis Magna mainly illustrate the Parthian campaigns, though we may wonder if they might also represent the appearance of the soldiers who destroyed the Garamantes in AD 202; the triumphal arch was erected in 203, when Severus visited his native city after that African campaign.

Cretan museums display little Roman military material. The stele of the cavalryman Tiberios Klaudios Roufos confirms the presence on the island of units of archers such as Cohors I Cretum Sagittariorum Equitata, but is too badly damaged to allow reconstruction of his appearance. His unit participated in Trajan's wars, and Levantine archers are represented on Trajan's Column with helmets of segmented construction, leather corselets and ringmail, and powerful composite bows.

BITHYNIA & PONTUS

Sculptures including images of Septimius Severus's legionaries again show the contemporary change in military dress (see Plate D2). Other monuments depict pseudo-Attic helmets (Nicomedia, Sinop), and the *thorax statos* (Agrilion/Adapazari). The stele of a local commander at Amasra also depicts his dog, and an axe (perhaps an attribute of the cult of Jupiter Dolichenus). Another statue there shows a muscled armour fitted with shoulder-doublings and decorated with a Nemesis motif on the breast; at the bottom edge what appears to be a metallic *cymation* has vegetal decoration, above a double range of *pteryges* which are repeated at the upper arms. Wearing a *paludamentum* cloak pinned at the left shoulder, this man was probably a general – perhaps even the *praefectus orae ponticae* of the local coastal unit, mentioned by Pliny the Younger (*Epist.*, X.21).

Military daggers are visible on the gravestones of cavalrymen, who are often depicted in scale armour and attended by a servant (*calo*). Others are shown wearing tunics while hunting with javelins or 'winged' spears, or protected by padded or quilted garments while fighting. The stelae confirm that the late Hellenistic practice of a horseman being accompanied by a servant bearing his spears and shield was continued among Greek units of the Roman army. Interestingly, one *calo* represented on a gravestone from Agrilion shows the main weapon as a double-headed axe (*bipennis*). On his stele from Samsun (ancient Amisos) the veteran decurion Gaius Numerius Maior is dressed in Parthian costume, including wide Persian *saravara* trousers, with a Roman dagger hanging from a baldric on his right side. This shows the degree of integration in material cultures; Numerius was probably a commander in an Eastern unit of archers or light cavalry (perhaps the Cohors Cypria). A terracotta statuette in Sinop Museum shows Parthian costume with a Phrygian cap.

A Buggenum-Montefortino helmet from Bithynia (Istanbul Archaeological Museum) is evidence of old models remaining in use until the end of the 1st century AD (and recalls that depicted on the Mikkalos monument). From Pontus, a pseudo-Attic helmet with a fronton of Hellenic type was found in a contemporary

Right side, and detached left cheek-guard, of a crushed Roman helmet of Hellenistic shape from Pontus, 1st century BC – 1st century AD; the comb is made of two matching flat plates sandwiched together. The helmet was found under a collapsed wall together with Roman coins of the Augustan period, but similar examples worn by Roman soldiers in various sculptures confirm the longevity of the Hellenistic tradition in Asia Minor. (Haluk Perk Müzesi, Istanbul; author's photo, courtesy of the Museum)

Damaged statue of a commander, early 1st century AD, from Aphrodisia, Asia. His splendid *thorax stadios* is decorated with a winged Nemesis motif on the upper chest, and with two opposing griffons partly obscured by the *zona militaris* sash. Just above this on the side (left) note one of the carefully sculpted D-rings, mounted in a decorative clasp, for lacing together the breast and back plates of the cuirass. (Aphrodisia Archaeological Museum; author's photos, courtesy of the Museum)

context between Sinop and Samsun. Helmets of such typology, worn by Roman senior officers visible on the Gemma Augustea, continued the Hellenistic tradition, especially in Asia Minor. A 1st-century masked helmet of Nijmegen-Kops Plateau type, once in the Guttmann Collection, probably came from north-west Turkey.

ASIA

One of the most important roles of Roman troops in this region, as throughout the Fertile Crescent, was policing; these provinces are therefore rich in representions of paramilitary personnel.

An example is the tombstone of Markos Aurelios Diodoros from Hierapolis (reconstructed as Plate E1); it is clear that such *diogmitai* or *parafylakes* performed both foot and mounted duties. This monument shows what seems to be a leather banded corselet (*corium*) worn over a thick *subarmalis*, medium-length javelins or spears, and the old Greek-type *machairas* curved, single-edged short-sword – rabbinical sources (*Midrash Tanhuma va-yehi 9*) confirm the persistence of this type in the East. Other images of light paramilitary corps from the first two centuries AD (Aphrodisia, Magnesia) represent men clearly dressed in Greek fashion, equipped only with spears and oval or small hexagonal shields, their waists again apparently protected by broad leather belting.

Ephesus, Halicarnassus (Bodrum), Aphrodisia, Aphyion, Smyrne (Izmir) and Hierapolis provide statues of senior commanders wearing helmets of pseudo-Corinthian type. Divinities are represented in various styles of *thorax stadios*, with greaves and crested helmets; the most impressive example is worn by Aeneas on the Sebasteion at Aphrodisia, which has shoulder-guards attached to lion's heads on the breast. The shield of Apollo is the Galatian variant of the Celtic *thureos*, as employed at that time in Thracia, Palestine, Asia Minor and Egypt.

Statuettes of cavalrymen show padded tunics and crested helmets, or Phrygian caps and long-sleeved tunics, worn sometimes with Eastern trousers (Aphyion, Canakkale Museum, Eskisehir, Usak-Ousakeion) and closed *calcei* shoes; some are armed with curved *machairai*. Stelae of cavalrymen usually show them unarmoured and attended by *calones*, some of whom have a Germanic appearance (Ephesus, Cyzicus), carrying their spears and shields (Aphyon, Canakkale Museums). Some cavalry tombstones from Eskisehir show the *parma* shield and *spatha* long-sword; others (Manisa-Magnesia) show cavalrymen in padded tunics armed with a double-headed axe or a hammer. The stele of a 1st-century AD officer who served in both Legiones IIII Scytica and V Macedonica clearly shows a typical *pugio*. A head of a soldier from Magnesia has a magnificent embossed pseudo-Attic helmet decorated with ram's horns, probably identifying him as a *cornicularius*.

Sarcophagi are also rich in details: pseudo-Corinthian helmets, circular shields (*aspides*) and muscled armours. The most striking is the 2nd-century sarcophagus of Claudius Severinus from Aizanoi, representing Greeks fighting Amazons. The costume of the Greeks is classical, but the specifics of armours, shoes, belts, shields and two

(continued on page 33)

DACIA
See commentary text for details

MOESIA SUPERIOR & INFERIOR
See commentary text for details

MACEDONIA, EPIRUS & ACHAIA
See commentary text for details

THRACIA, BITHYNIA & PONTUS
See commentary text for details

D

ASIA, GALATIA & CYPRUS
See commentary text for details

LYCIA-PAMPHILIA, CILICIA & CRETA
See commentary text for details

F

SYRIA, JUDAEA & CAPPADOCIA
See commentary text for details

AEGYPTUS, ARABIA & CYRENAICA
See commentary text for details

different types of masked helmets suggest that the artist studied contemporary Roman equipment closely.

Bronze armour-scales from the Bodrum area, now in Istanbul's Haluk Perk Museum, show one hole for fastening to the backing and two at the sides through which they are still fastened together horizontally with wire; each measured 2.5cm x 1.7cm (0.98in x 0.66 in). Among newly excavated items are a beautifully made bronze *draco* standard head from the Tralleis region (Aydin Museum), and three fragments of *cornua* (horns – musical instruments) now in the Eskisehir-Dorylaeum Museum.

GALATIA

Auxiliary cohorts in this province fulfilled a variety of essential tasks, such as carrying messages, guarding Imperial officials, patrolling the roads and gathering supplies. Their numbers are likely to have been small, however, and inscriptions indicate that they tended to concentrate in the province's capital, Ancyra (today's Ankara) or at other strategic sites.

The Hellenized Celts living in Galatian territory were now cavalrymen in Roman service. The Museum of Anatolian Civilizations has 1st – 2nd-century sculptures representing military commanders with Phrygian helmets and muscled armours, worn over sleeved tunics and long trousers echoing Celtic types. Stelae of cavalrymen represent them in padded 'striped' tunics, or standing with composite armour and spear. Fragmentary statues show *crepidae* on the feet of soldiers. Interestingly, a silver mirror with a mythological scene shows an early example of the employment of a war mace. Bronze statuettes of Ares (Mars) show muscled armours and pseudo-Corinthian helmets fitted with high plumes; terracotta statuettes show cavalry with sleeved tunics and long trousers (Isparta), and guards with swords and round shields (Burdur Museum, finds from ancient Limnombria and Sagalassos). An interesting detail on a sarcophagus from Konya depicts a club fitted with a wrist-loop; a relief from Büyük Kale represents a 'policeman' on horseback and his companions armed with clubs or short staffs and round shields, wearing cloaks wrapped out of their way around their waists.

The only military artefact in the Ankara archaeological museum is a single glass *phalera* with the image of Germanicus, though the collection also boasts a signet ring with the inscription of Legio V, and cameos with representations of armours, standards and a warship. Recent excavations at Gordion have recovered decorative brooches of the bow type, and inset-enameled tail-in-mouth 'snakes' (parallels from Raetia). Excavations between 1993 and 2002 yielded large quantities of military finds including iron and bronze armour scales, and many mail rings; a javelin head, and a triangular-headed bronze Roman arrowhead; and medallions and pendants such as were commonly worn as military decorations. Julian Bennett, trench supervisor of the work, believes that the dimensions of the excavated conjoining rooms are directly comparable with those found in Roman legionary and auxiliary barracks of the 1st – 2nd centuries AD; it is therefore possible that Gordion is the first Roman auxiliary camp found and excavated in Turkey.

LYCIA & PAMPHYLIA

Funerary images of cavalrymen now in various museums of this province show conical caps in Hellenic style (Telmessos-Fethiye) and short tunics,

Detail of the Aphrodisia statue (see page 24), showing the elaborate *crepidae* footwear with criss-cross strapping down the instep. The pseudo-Boeotian helmet at the general's feet has a broad, fluted brim, a diadem-like fronton, and a long horsehair plume that retains traces of red colour. The item at top right is not part of the helmet, but a corner of the general's cloak. (Aphtodisia Archaeological Museum; author's photos, courtesy of the Museum)

sometimes folded and padded (Antalya Museum), with only the belt revealing military status. A plaque in the latter museum shows a commander with a pseudo-Attic helmet of Thracian style, probably an Anatolian cavalry officer in the Roman army during the late 1st century BC or early 1st century AD. Sarcophagi show composite bows, pseudo-Attic helmets, and many leather corselets worn by infantry (Side Museum, Antalya Museum) and cavalry (see Plate F1). The armour of the monster Geryon on the 'Sarcophagus of Herakles' from Perge is represented as a metal *thorax stadios*, worn with Greek boots, and javelins and round shields are also depicted.

A statue of Herakles shows a beautiful quiver with the feather fletchings visible (Antalya). Round, embossed shields are seen on some statues, like the one dedicated by Claudios Peison to Aphrodite (Perge). Again from Perge, a frieze shows many military items including rectangular and oval legionary shields paralleled on Antonine monuments. Statuettes of Mars show muscled armour and pseudo-Corinthian helmets.

While artefacts are scarce, the Alanya Museum has three bronze fragments from a veteran auxiliary infantryman's discharge diploma, from the city of Laertes. It records the recipient's name, his city of origin (Cyrrhos in Syria), his unit, the names of his commander and of the governor of Pamphylia, and the date of issue (AD 138). From Caria, the Halik Perk Museum has an interesting 2nd-century AD socketed *pilum* shank 82cm (32.3ins) long, with an elongated 'bodkin' head, and incorporating a small sphere about 19cm (7.5ins) above the socket – perhaps for balance?

CILICIA

Several sources mention Cilicians in Roman army units, or as *stationarii*, i.e. garrison troops recruited locally to defend outposts and police strategic

Front and rear views of a section of bronze scale armour, early 2nd century AD, from Gordion in Galatia. Among numerous scales and mail rings excavated in 2005, this impressive assembly of 13 scales overlapped from right to left was still linked together by its original loops of copper-alloy wire. Traces of leather on the back of the *squamae* may be the remains of the original backing material. (Drawing by Dr Andrei Negin)

5 cm

roads, harbours and frontiers like Artanada. It is highly probable that the crude military stelae carved into rocks in various locations (Adamkalayar, Veyselli, Çanakçi, Kizkalesi) represent such soldiers, presumably from the 2nd century AD. These images are unarmoured but carry weapons, mainly a javelin (*akontion*) and the short sword, invariably worn on the left from a baldric over the right shoulder. The shape of the sword is clearly of Pompeii typology (but see variation, Plate F3). The tunics are closed at the waist by a knotted sash or cloth belt, and the *sagum* military cloak is also depicted; footwear are invariably short boots, similar to those found in the Egyptian fort of Dydimoi.

Among other military sculptures in the province, the stele of a cavalryman from Silifke shows a wide case for javelins or bow-and-arrows on the horse's right side. Fragments of sarcophagi (Mersin) show pseudo-Attic helmets and muscled armours. Hunting-scene mosaics show composite bows and winged spears (Adana). There have been finds of staff *fibulae* of the 1st – 2nd centuries, and arrowheads.

Monument to a Cilician warrior in Roman service, 2nd century AD, from the rock graves at Çanakçi; compare with Plate F3. As well as his spear, this is one of the several soldiers represented as carrying the Roman *dolabra* pickaxe; this might suggest their employment as marine troops, since many Cilicians took service as *classiari* with the fleet, where such axes were employed as weapons. (*in situ*; photo courtesy Dick Osseman)

CAPPADOCIA

This extremely militarized province extended to Pontus and the Black Sea. Notwithstanding the limited archaeological investigation, such finds as do exist give the impression of an important Roman army presence.

Legionary bow-brooches are preserved from the provincial capital Kayseri and from Amasya (ancient Amasea-Merzifon). Military decorations of Medusa shape, and appliqués from armour, are preserved in Amasya and Giresun, with both tanged and socketed arrowheads.

Figurative monuments include sarcophagi depicting pseudo-Attic helmets and round shields, muscled armours, bows, arrows and double-headed axes. The site of Satala, permanent fortress of Legio XVI Flavia Firma and later of XV Apollinaris, has yielded stelae of legionaries. Weapons have also been found, but their size, number and typology are unpublished.

COLCHIS & BOSPHORUS

Although finds of Roman military equipment on the northern coasts of the Black Sea are extremely rare, they do confirm the other evidence of a Roman military presence. An important bronze helmet was unearthed in Kvemo Kedi village (Dedoplistskaro Museum); despite its very bad condition, Bishop and Coulston classify it as an Imperial Gallic (Weisenau) type, and propose a date between AD 25 and the Flavian period. A similar helmet from the mid- or second half of the 1st century AD came from Sochi. Fragments of an Imperial Gallic Type I helmet (1st century BC – 1st century AD) were found near the sanctuary at Gurzufskoe Sedlo pass. Other finds from Crimea and Kuban include a *pilum* of the 1st century BC – 1st century AD discovered near Vozdvizhenskaya village; the top of a standard (village of Tiflis, right bank of the Kuban); bone chapes of *spatha* scabbards, *c.* AD 150–200, from Tyra, Olbia and Chersonesus; and the crossguard of a Roman sword from the village of Tenghinka.

Other unmistakably Roman finds from the Chersonese have included: two harness *phalerae* (late 1st – early 2nd century AD); the indented bone grip from a Pompeii sword; a decorated *pugio* sheath (parallels from

Roman Imperial Gallic helmet from Sochi on the Black Sea coast of south-west Russia, 1st century AD. This was an area under Roman influence, and sometimes direct control. (Sochi Archaeological Museum; drawing by Dr Andrei Negin)

Two helmets from Nawa, Syria, 1st – 2nd century AD.

(Left) Silvered bronze mask, with embossed and engraved moustache and long, curled sideboards in the Eastern fashion.
(Centre) The complete helmet, with mask in place; the skull is hammered and drawn down from a single piece of bronze, very skilfully embossed overall with figures including a sun deity, eagles, a winged Victory, a warrior, four-horse chariots, oval shields and trophies of armour.

(Right) The second, open-face helmet; of rather thicker metal than the first, this has smaller embossed figures including Medusa, an eagle, generals, a Roman/Parthian battle scene showing ringmail and pseudo-Attic helmets, groups of figures flanking a sacrificial altar, and Mars and Minerva. (Drawings by Dr Andrei Negin, courtesy National Museum, Damascus)

Vindonissa, not later than AD 50); a sword scabbard chape of Mainz typology; a *pelta*-shaped bronze and iron buckle from a *cingulum* (Type A, Deschler-Erb classification) excavated in the ancient port, and perhaps of Tiberian-Neronian date (parallel in Valkenburg, AD 40–69); and a bronze hook from an armour of Corbridge type, with a preserved copper rivet, attached to a metal plate about 1mm thick (Type 4, Thomas classification).

Objects from an important private collection are also noteworthy. A palmette appliqué from a Pompeii scabbard found in Charax has a parallel in a similar ornament found at Bori in the Caucasus, and others in Linz. It may be associated with the Crimean campaign of Plautius Silvanus, governor of Taurica; apparently, the first Romans to enter Charax were soldiers of Legio VIII Augusta and sailors of the Classis Ravennatis. In the autumn of AD 69 the VIII Augusta was transferred to Syria, to be replaced by Legio I Italica; a generation later the manpower demands of the Dacian wars forced a partial or complete withdrawal of the Charax garrison.

Fragments of edge-gutter from a Pompeii sword scabbard were found in the sanctuary at the pass of Gurzufskoe Sedlo, as well as ten pieces of iron ringmail of four types (using riveted, butted and solid rings of 5.5–9.5mm (0.22–0.37in) outer diameter); a large fragment of fine bronze mail; and iron edge-binding from an early-Principate rectangular *scutum*. Novichenkova dated all Roman finds at Gurzufskoe Sedlo to the Roman–Bosphoran war of AD 45–49, but the presence of a Pompeii sword that early is debatable. Another Pompeii-type scabbard fragment came from Krasnozorensky; comparison of these finds with others from Aquincum and Vindonissa has led some scholars to propose that Legiones VIII Augusta and VII Claudia, and their subordinate auxiliary cohorts, took part in Plautius Silvanus's campaign. Part of a bronze helmet from the Ust-Alma necropolis has been similarly dated. The private collection also includes two wire-connected *squamae* of the Antonine period from Charax, and others in iron and bronze were found during excavation of a Roman post on the Kasankoj height.

SYRIA

A marvellous masked helmet from the royal necropolis at Homs (Emesa) probably belonged to a member of the royal family of that allied kingdom,

only incorporated into the Empire in AD 78. This is the first mask-helmet to reveal the attachment of mask to skull by straps fastened with a buckle at the rear above the neck-guard.

A second important military assemblage came from the grave at Nawa of a Roman senior officer, probably a commander in Trajan's war against the Parthians (see Plate G2). This contained two highly decorated helmets, a scale armour, various weapons, and richly decorated bronze, silvered and gilded elements of horse harness including an articulated chamfron with side plates.

The cities of Zeugma and Antiochia ad Taurum yielded *fibulae,* round appliqués from the *cymation* of corselets, sling-bullets, a ring-pommel sword of the late 2nd century AD, and a 2nd-century cheek-piece from a decorated pseudo-Attic helmet embossed with Nemesis (Glass Museum, Gaziantep). The American Institute in Beirut has lion-shaped shield bosses of the Severan period, and tanged bodkin arrowheads particularly suited for penetrating armour.

There are vastly too many artworks in the province to list here. They show muscled armours in metal and leather with a wide range of different arrangements of *cymation* and *pteryges,* and in one case a depiction of a servant lacing a corselet at the side. There are helmets of pseudo-Attic and pseudo-Corinthian forms, spears, javelins, *gladii* and *parazonia* swords, and Zeus armed with a *bipennis* axe. Garments include *paludamenta,* sleeved tunics and trousers. The 2nd-century 'Four Seasons' mosaic in Antioch shows blue *exomis* tunics leaving one shoulder bare, off-white tunics with red *clavi* worn with a yellow-bordered blue *sagum,* and *lacernae* cloaks. Footwear include *calcei* and *cothurni* boots, and 'netted' *campagi raeticulati.* Richly detailed sculptures show Rome's allied Palmyrene generals and their troops. The former display Greco-Roman fashions, while the latter wear Parthian-Iranian long-sleeved tunics and *saravara* trousers, and carry bows, decorated bow-cases, long spears, swords, and small round shields.

CYPRUS

From Palaepaphos, a signet ring belonging to a centurion of Legio XV Apollinaris attests the passage of the future emperor Titus in AD 69. Among few military relics of the early Principate in Cypriot museums are bronze arrowheads from various localities (Kato Paphos); an iron sword showing a local evolution of the *falcata* (House of Dionysos, Nea Paphos); and a socketed *pilum* (Cyprus Museum, Nicosia).

JUDAEA

We owe our extensive knowledge of Roman equipment used in Palestine to three factors: ancient sources (the *Bellum Judaicum* of Josephus, and Jewish and Christian texts); the major Israeli archaeological excavations of sites with dateable contexts, pertinent to the First and Second Revolts; and the preservative effects of the arid climate. Again, space prevents detailed discussion here, but the work by Dr Guy Stiebel (see Bibliography) is recommended. One general lesson is the mixture of Roman and Eastern elements employed.

An astonishing discovery in 1982, under collapsed stones at Gamala on the Golan Heights, was the named equipment of Lucius Magus, perhaps a soldier of Legio V Macedonica. It included the cast copper-alloy

Terracotta statuette of an Eastern Roman cavalryman from Lebanon (Syria), late 2nd century AD. Note the Phrygian-style helmet typical of the Severan period, the scale armour and oval shield. (American University Museum, Beirut; author's photo, courtesy of the Museum)

Fragment from a 1st-century AD fresco from Kato Paphos, Cyprus, showing an archer seating an arrow against his bowshaft. The detail of his grip is interesting, with the arrow lying across the web of his thumb and passing between the first two fingers rather than on top of the index finger. (Paphos District Museum; author's photo, courtesy of the Museum)

Detail of the scabbard chape of a Pompeii *gladius*, 1st century AD, from Jerusalem. Miniature inscriptions and images on the chape suggest that it was awarded to a centurion of Legio V Macedonica for leading a cohort at Lake Tiberias (aka the Sea of Galilee) in September AD 67. (David Xavier Collection; owner's photo)

cheek-pieces and a brow-guard, both tinned, from a Coolus-Hagenau helmet (Coolus Type G in Robinson's classification). Large fragments of a *lorica segmentata* had the three upper back plates fastened in a way quite different from the Corbridge specimens (the Novae fragments had already hinted at such a system). Briefly, the plates were united not by leather straps but by stud-like rivets sliding along slots in overlapping plates. Some plates had rounded corners, as visible on Trajan's Column. Copper-alloy fittings from laminated cuirasses were also found in Samaria, at Masada, Kh. Khumran, Jerusalem, Legio and Jotapata. The Gamala finds also included a fragment of a *manica* or *galerus*; this, and another in copper alloy from Camp F at Masada, confirmed that articulated right-arm armour was not an innovation of the later Dacian wars.

Scale armour was widespread, often made in copper alloy, and in the 1st century AD (but not the 2nd) usually with a raised mid-rib. Some 1,090 bronze scales, plated in brass and silver colours, were found at Masada, but only one iron example. By contrast, a complete cuirass unearthed at Sepphoris and associated with the Second Revolt was made of iron scales without mid-ribs; its rows were not attached to each other, but directly to an organic backing. Copper-alloy scales were found at Wadi el Mafjer, Bethther (Second Revolt), By-pass Shoa'm and Megiddo, and a complete 2nd-century section of 13 rows of a collar or shoulder-guard in Sarmatian style was recovered near Legio. Stiebel identifies 15 different types of scales (sometimes more than one used in the same armour); generally they overlap from right to left, on a fabric backing. Initially they fastened through two holes to adjacent scales, but in the 2nd century four holes in each scale were used for sewing to the backing, and the side holes for fastening to adjacent scales.

Fragments of ringmail came from Masada, and a complete armour from the Hebron hoard had a fastening disc for shoulder-doublings. This mailshirt was made of welded rings interwoven in fours, with a bottom hemline formed from iron scales. The same site yielded pieces of copper-alloy greaves. Fragments of composite armour (iron mail covered with small *plumata* copper-alloy scales) were found in the siege level in Jerusalem. Importantly, the Jewish *Tosefta Kelim Baba Metzia* (T. Kel BM 3.1) also provides an explicit reference to leather armour of segmental construction, divided horizontally.

Poplar shield-boards of the Second Revolt period were recovered at the Sandal Cave (one with white gesso on leather facing, painted in red and black); at the Pool Cave (from an earlier oval shield, with leather binding or facing); and at Gamala, together with an iron-bar handle, as well as the copper-alloy *tabula ansata* named to Lucius Magus. Gamala also yielded two identical circular copper-alloy bosses from auxiliary shields, and some copper-alloy edge-binding.

At least ten fragmentary shields were found at Masada, some suggesting that cohorts painted them in different colours: three crimson-red examples, and one azure-blue. The Masada finds suggest that both sides of shields were faced with leather; we may note that both Martial (*Epigr.*,VII, 2, 1–2) and Ovid (*Met.*, 13, 347) use the word *tergum* for a shield coated with layers of leather. The three main types found at Masada were:

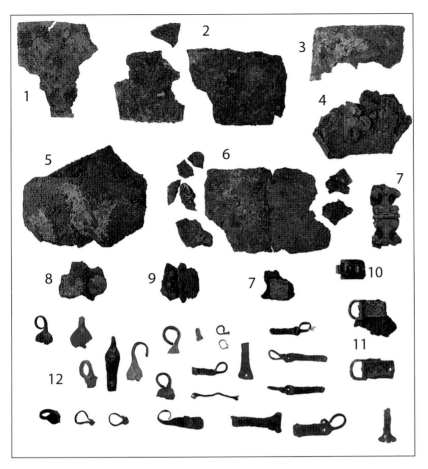

Although no details can be made out at this scale, this 'jigsaw puzzle' is in itself a tribute to the work of Israeli archaeologists. It shows (1–6) the fragments of the important *lorica segmentata* of Lucius Magus found at Gamala, including iron backplate fragments with a sliding mechanism, (7–9) yellow-metal lobate hinges, and (10–12) D-buckles and tie-loops, several of the latter riveted closed. (Drawings by Dr Andrei Negin, ex-Stiebel)

(1) The rectangular *scutum*, with slightly rounded corners and leather edging, made of three layers of plywood covered on both sides with painted goat-leather. (The site of Aro'er' also provided an example of the copper-alloy hemispherical boss typical of the rectangular *scutum*, with a rectangular flange pierced with seven holes for attachment by dome-headed rivets.)

(2) A variant of (1) made of plywood planks, coated with palmleaf fibre perhaps as a basis for the glued-on leather facing, and with copper-alloy gutter edging.

(3) An oval cavalry shield made of relatively thick planks with leather binding, as also found at Nahal David (Second Revolt).

As to helmets, apart from the Coolus find from Gamala we have the famous 2nd-century AD iron Imperial Italic Type G from the Hebron hoard, with crossed skull-bars like the Berzobis specimen, and copper-alloy crescent moon decorations and edge-guttering; and an 'Alexander' mask-helmet, the iron bowl bearing a copper-alloy wreath. Fragmentary finds on many sites attest the presence of the Weiler-type cavalry helmet (Masada); the Imperial Gallic Type A/Weisenau legionary helmet (Masada Camp F, Legio X Fretensis); the Imperial Italic, with soldered-on ear-guards (Gamala); a late 2nd-century pseudo-Attic 'sports' helmet (Gamala – parallels with Theilenhofen specimen); and a 2nd-century pseudo-Attic helmet with decorations recalling those of the Praetorian Guards (Jerusalem).The prominence of yellow-metal helmets in the 1st century AD is evident.

Arrowheads – leaf-shaped, trilobate, flat, of rhomboid or square section, and bodkin; of iron, bronze, copper alloy, and bone; socketed or tanged – have been found on many sites. There is evidence for the use of ibex bone in the construction of bows, and of both lead and stone sling-bullets.

Fragments of typical *pugio* daggers and copper-alloy sheath fittings have been recovered at Jotapata, Gamala, Ein-Gedi and Masada. Long oriental daggers are known from Masada and Kalgouia, and leather scabbards from the Caves complex. Another long, narrow, double-edged dagger (34.5cm/13.6ins) found at Mo'a probably belonged to a Nabatean auxiliary. A 1st-century AD Pompeii-type *gladius* was found in its scabbard in a water culvert in Jerusalem; 93cm long overall, it has a flat oval-section 73cm blade (36.6 and 28.7 ins). The leather-faced plywood scabbard, with three transverse decorated copper-alloy bands, has iron edge-guttering and two pairs of attachment rings. A sword of Mainz typology (59.6cm/23.4ins long) was also excavated in the upper city, and dated to AD 70. Another blade of the same type was found at Masada, among many sword and scabbard fragments of both Mainz and Pompeii typology, including red-painted leather from a scabbard decorated with delicate open-work. Masada also yielded bone and ivory handgrips from four *spathae*.

Among shafted weapons, legionary *pilum* heads were found in Samaria (square cross-section head), Yoqne'am (bodkin head), Gamala (two collets), Kh. Qumran, Bethther (socketed), Nahal Yattir (socketed, Second Revolt), Wadi Murabba'ât (slightly pyramid-section tanged head), and Nahal Ever (collared head, Second Revolt). *Hasta* spearheads and some ferrules have been found at Jericho (besieged by Vespasian in AD 68), Jotapata, Gamala (second half of 1st century BC), By-Pass Shoa'm, Masada, Wadi Murabba'ât, and Khirbet El Aqd (Second Revolt). One of the most interesting finds from Gamala is a *falx muralis* (see Plate G1). Josephus writes (*BJ,* III, 5, 96) that horsemen had 'a long pole *[kontos]* in their hand… [and] on one side of their horses… three or more darts *[akontes]* are borne in their quiver, having broad points, and not smaller than spears'. A broad-bladed javelin came from Wadi Suweinit (Second Revolt); a light 2nd-century cavalry javelin from the Caves complex (Madbach Sa'yid Abidah); and the 7cm (2.75in) flat, rounded leaf-shaped heads of Nabatean *mizraq* javelins from Kurnub, Tell-Shalem and Ein Rachel.

Many hobnails from *caligae* of the 1st – 2nd centuries have been found in Samaria, Jericho, Masada, Jotapata, Jerusalem, Gamala, the Sandal Cave, the Large Caves complex, Kh.Qumran, Tel Shalem, Legio, Wadi Suweinit, Ein-Gedi, Kh. Al Salantah, Nahal Yattir, and Kh.Hillel. Belt fittings and pendants, some decorated or silvered, and copper-alloy or bone sheath-attachments, are almost as common. A Nabatean girth buckle came from Ein Rachel, together with the earrings of a Nabatean archer.

The rarest finds of all are the fragments of tunics and other garments from Masada (white and red *tunicae*, and *sagum* of Gallic manufacture), and from the Bar Kochba caves. That red was characteristic of the Roman army may be inferred from the fact that the Jews called them *edom* because of their red garments. The cloak in which the soldiers dressed the mocked Christ was described by St Matthew (XVII, 27–29) as a bright

Gladius of Pompeii type, AD 66, from Jerusalem. In 2011 this well-preserved sword and parts of its belt, dating from the First Jewish Revolt, were found in an ancient drainage tunnel. With a 73cm (28.7in) blade, it still had its leather-faced scabbard with some intact decoration. (Photo courtesy Israel Antiquity Authority)

red *chlamys* (*kokkīnos*); St Mark speaks of a 'common purple' (XV, 16–17), and St John of a purple *himàtion* (XIX, 2). This may suggest that auxiliary soldiers in Judaea – or at least their officers – had 'purple' cloaks, but in fact we cannot know exactly what shade was being described. In the ancient world true purple dye from the murex mollusc was much more expensive than the red vegetable dyes normally used. Depending upon context, the term might in fact refer to a range of shades from violet to bright red, or even red-brown (see also page 42).

As in other provinces, troops in Judaea probably adopted items of local clothing. Jewish garments of the Hellenistic/ Herodian style were in yellow, green, black, red and white, decorated with vertical stripes and notch-ended bands. They were draped in a particular way, and often had decorative fringes. Hellenistic sandals and laced boots would have been worn alongside *caligae*.

ARABIA

The Arabian Nabateans fought for the Romans against the Jewish rebels, and the archaeology and the sources suggest both light infantry and mounted warriors. The camel was their most distinctive feature, and from representations of *dromedarii* troops we can glean details of Nabatean equipment.

Offensive weapons were mainly those of ancient local provenance: slings and bows. Warriors – probably *dromedarii* and cavalry armed with a long spear (as on the Hadhebt el-Hamra relief) – are described in rabbinical sources (*Tosefta Taanit, 28b*) as armed with a long, heavy spear (*romach*) and light throwing javelins (*mizrāq, mizraqah*). Reliefs from Petra and Kerak show ribbed spearheads. A composite bow is visible on a *putto* from Siq El Barid, with bent stiffeners. A flat, leaf-shaped iron tanged arrowhead from Israel belonged to Nabatean auxiliaries. Short daggers shown slung on camel saddles are of Roman type, with three-lobe pommels, shouldered blades, and sheaths with gutter frames, two suspension loops and a bulbous terminal.

The Arabian *deitzah*, a small Nabatean targe shield made of gazelle hide, is mentioned in the Mishnah and is visible in *dromedarii* sculptures. Perhaps 38cm (15ins) in diameter, it lacked a boss, but was sometimes reinforced with four rivets arranged decoratively. Generally Arabian warriors went unarmoured. However, reliefs from Petra show helmets and muscled cuirasses on gravestones of Roman soldiers, and oval and round shields. A pair of vertical fasteners from a Newstead-type *lorica segmentata* were found in the Romano-Nabatean fortress of Ein Rachel. One decorated sports helmet from the Jordan (see page 6) is similar to the one probably represented on the stele of Maris Casitilius of the Ala Parthorum et Araborum from Mainz.

AEGYPTUS

Romano-Egyptian military men are immortalized in the hauntingly lifelike full-colour funerary portraits from El-Fayyoum. They are represented in their red or white uniforms (the latter, *tunicae albae*), sometimes decorated with red or

Detail from a stele that provides a rare representation of a Roman *dromedarius* of the 2nd century AD. These camel-mounted units were created by Trajan to operate in the desert areas of Arabia Petrea and Judaea. Note, right of his head, the spearhead with a curved lateral extension like a *falx muralis* – compare with Plate G1. (Musei Capitolini, Rome; photo courtesy Dr Marina Mattei)

Fragments of banded leather armour, 2nd century AD, from Kasr Ibrahim. This puzzling item might be part of a leather cuirass, such as the wide belt-like protection visible on the gravestone of Aurelios Diodoros – see Plate E1. (British Museum; author's photo, courtesy of the Museum)

Statuette of a lightly equipped infantryman – *levis armatura* – of the 2nd century AD. (Egyptian Museum, Cairo; author's photo, courtesy of the Museum)

purple *clavi*; their cloaks are blue *chlamydes* or red-brown *saga*; and in two cases we can see studded pinkish-red *subarmales*. They carry *gladii* slung from *cingula bullata* (baldrics studded with bosses) of crimson or dark brown colour.

Warrior statuettes now in Cairo Museum represent mainly light infantry, but statues of armoured notables also survive; for example, an armoured torso in the Alexandria National Museum shows the cuirass with the common embossed or applied Nemesis motif on the breast, and a very detailed representation of a phoenix below the *zona militaris*. The same museum has a sculpted head wearing a pseudo-Attic helmet, which seems to have been the favoured style in this province.

Fragments of a wooden shield decorated with studs have been found at Kasr Ibrim, together with slingstones, bodkin arrowheads, cane shafts and one complete with head, probably a local production. Many *caligae* and *calcei* military footwear have been found. The old excavations by Flinders-Petrie yielded camp tools (axes, hoes, chains), and weapons, e.g. arrowheads with heavy squared heads from Dodona, fighting knives, and the ribbed handgrip of a *gladius* from Defenna. The 'helmet of Sheik Ibada' from Antinoopolis (1st – 2nd centuries AD) is a 'sports' type, lavishly decorated with images of griffins.

Rubbish deposits on the sites of *praesidia* have provided quantities of textile and leather fragments which shed new light on the Roman army's dye sources and dyeing technology. The iconography includes representations of common soldiers wearing various shades of purple, and textile finds include those with a purple ground, or with woven decorations including weft threads dyed in a broad range of shades ranging from greyish-mauve to dark violet. Analysis of 13 finds from Maximianon, Krokodilô and Didymoi revealed the alternative dyestuffs and processes used to produce the cheaper imitations; however, some finds showed the true 'Tyrian' purple obtained from marine molluscs. This argues that even the most expensive dye might be available to the lower classes, military and civilian; from Dios and Xeron came fragments of woven-to-shape semicircular hooded cloaks decorated with applied woven bands in true purple. Didymoi also yielded a complete specimen of felt and wool *galericulum* or under-helmet, and various military headgears from Mons Claudianus included a woollen 'pillbox' prototype of the later *pilleus pannonicus*.

These sites also provided large numbers of military footwear: *calcei* (with open vamp), and early *campagi militares*, some of them of sophisticated design and fitted with hobnails. Some specimens of military *soleae* sandals had inner soles cut shaped to the toes and unshaped outsoles, these and the straps being cut from a single piece of leather. Specimens of 2nd-century *perones* cavalry boots from Didymoi had high, stiff, closed shafts like those of much later periods.

MESOPOTAMIA

Several artworks represent the legions which invaded and garrisoned this province under Trajan. The Ephesus casket shows legionaries, praetorians, *equites singulares* and *speculatores* clad in tunics, ringmail fitted with shoulder-doubling, muscled corselets worn over padded *subarmales*, and pseudo-Attic helmets decorated with incised laurel wreaths. The shield blazons recall those of Legiones XII Fulminata and V Macedonica, which took part in the Armenian campaign.

The celebration of Lucius Verus's campaigns in Parthia is illustrated on another Ephesus monument, where young Asian warriors (under the command of the legate Avidius Cassius of Legio III Gallica) fight the Parthians clad only in pseudo-Attic helmets and *exomis* tunics and armed with sword and shield.

On Septimius Severus's triumphal arch at Leptis Magna in Cyrenaica, a depiction of his siege of the Parthian city of Ctesiphon, *c.* AD 195, shows a *testudo* of shields; close study also reveals a legionary wearing both the *lorica segmentata* and an articulated *manica* arm-protector, as more usually associated with Trajan's Dacian campaigns nearly a century earlier. The Arch of Severus in Rome's Forum shows soldiers with the same equipment as represented in Leptis Magna, with more details such as *paenulae*, *saga*, *lacernae* and *caligae*. However, amongst the legionaries are represented groups of soldiers surrounding the Emperor who, although dressed partially in Eastern garb, have typical Roman *focales* scarves, dagged-edge ringmail or flexible leather *loricae*, *subarmales*, short *feminalia* breeches, and *carbatinae* interlaced shoes. Baldrics to the right hip support a kind of semi-*spatha*, and on the left they carry small round shields, but their most unusual item is a Phrygian helmet or cap. Scholars have identified them variously as Danubian bodyguards of the Emperor (*SHA*, Max. Duo, III, 5), Eastern auxiliaries, or soldiers of the new created Legio II Parthica. A splendid gilded Phrygian helmet from Mesopotamia is now in the Museum of Fine Arts, Boston.

Equites of the army of Septimius Severus campaigning against the Parthians in Mesopotamia, end of the 2nd century AD. Note the pseudo-Attic helmet, and the long coat of mail worn over an arming jerkin whose short *pteryges* are only visible for a few inches above the tunic hem. (Archaeological Museum, Leptis Magna; photo courtesy Luca Bonacina)

SELECT BIBLIOGRAPHY

Note: For reasons of space, we can list here only the ancient sources and some of the most relevant modern works. A much fuller bibliography of the academic publications, in several languages, can be found on the Osprey website by following: www.ospreypublishing.com/maa_511_bibliography

Ancient sources

Apuleius, *The Golden Ass, or a Book of Changes*, ed. J.C. Relihan (Indianapolis & Cambridge, 2007)

Arrianus, Flavius, *Scripta minora*, ed. R. Hercher & A. Ehehard (Lipsiae, 1887)

The Holy Bible, Old and New Testaments, translated out of the original tongues, ed. Thomas & Sons (New York, 1901)

Josephus, *The Works of Josephus* (BJ), ed. W. Whiston (Peabody, 1987)

I Manoscritti di Qumran, ed. L. Moraldi (Turin, 1971)

Marci Fabii Quintiliani Declamationes, apud Seb. Gryphius (Lyon, 1540); Latin and English text in The Orator's Education, V, Books 11–12, Quintilian, in Loeb Classical Library (Harvard University Press, 2002)

Martial, *Epigrams*, Vol. II, Books 6–10 (Harvard University Press, 1993)

The Midrash on Psalms, vol. 13 (1–2), ed. L. Nemoy, S. Lieberman, H.A. Wolfson & W.B. Braude (Yale University Press, 1959)

Midrash Rabbah to Exodus (Ex. R.) in H. Freedman & M. Simon, Midrash Rabbah, Vol. III (London & Bournemouth, 1951)

Midrash Rabbah to Lamentations (Ex. R.) in H. Freedman & M. Simon, Midrash Rabbah, Vol. VII (London & Bournemouth, 1951)

Midrash Tanḥuma, ed. S. Buber (Vilna, 1885– in Hebrew)

Mishnah, ed. W. Romm & Bros (Vilna, 1913)

Ovid, *Metamorphoses*, Books IX–XV (Harvard University Press, 1916)

Pausanias, *Description of Greece (Per.)*, Vols VIII 22–X (Loeb Classical Library, Harvard University Press, 1935)

Pliny the Elder, *Natural History – Historia Naturalis* (HN), 10 vols (Harvard University Press, 1938–62)

Pliny the Younger, *Complete Letters – Epistulae* (Ep.) (Oxford University Press, 1996)

Plutarch, *Parallel Lives*, 11 vols (Harvard University Press, 1914–26)

Scriptores Historia Augusta (SHA), 3 vols (Harvard University Press, 1921–32)

Scrivener, F.H.A., *The New Testament in the Original Greek according to the Text followed in the Authorised Version* (Cambridge, 1894)

Tacitus, IV, *Annals* 4–6, 11–12 (Loeb Classical Library, Harvard University Press, 1937)

The Talmud of the Land of Israel, Vol. I, ed. J. Neusner (Chicago, 1989)

Tosefta, ed. R.S. Zuckermandel & S. Lieberman (Jerusalem, 1970)

The Tosefta, translated from the Hebrew, 6 vols, ed. J. Neusner (New York,1977–86)

Tosefta Avodah Zarah, ed. F.C. Ewald (Nurberg, 1856)

Tosefta Kelim Baba Metzia in S. Lieberman, Tosefta, Vol. III (Jerusalem, 1966)

Tosefta Sotah in S. Lieberman, Tosefta, Nashim 2 (New York, 1973)

Modern works

Abdul-Hak, S., 'Rapport préliminaire sur des objets provenant de la nécropole romaine située a proximité de Nawa (Hauran)' in *Les Annales Archéologiques de Syrie* (1954–55, 4–5),163–188

Bishop, M.C. & J.C.N. Coulston, *Roman Military Equipment, from the Punic Wars to the Fall of Rome* (London, 1993)

Cermanovic Kuzmanovic, A., & A. Jovanovic, *Tekija* (Belgrade, 2004)

Cheesman, G.L., *The Auxilia of the Roman Imperial Army* (Oxford, 1914)

Chiarucci, P., *Settimio Severo e la Legione Seconda Partica* (Albano Laziale, 2006)

Cuvigny, H. (ed.), *La Route de Myos Hormos – L'Armée romaine dans le désert Oriental d'Egypte* (Cairo, 2003)

D'Amato, R., *Arms and Armour of the Imperial Roman Soldier, from Marius to Commodus, 112 BC–192 AD* (London, 2009)

Etienne, R., I. Piso & A. Diaconescu, 'Le fouilles du Forum Vetus de Sarmizegetusa' in *AMN*, 39–40:1 (2002–3), 59–86

Gentscheva, E., 'Neuen Angeben Bezuglich des Militarlagers von Novae im Unterdonaubecken aus der fruheren Kaiserzeit' in *AB*, 3 (1999), 21–33

Goldman, A., 'From Phrygian capital to rural fort, new evidence for Roman military at Gordion, in Turkey', in *Penn Museum Expedition Magazine*, No. 3, Vol. 49, 6–12

Haynes, I*., Blood of the Provinces. The Roman Auxilia and the Making of Provincial Society from Augustus to the Severans* (Oxford, 2014)

Hoti. A., *Épidamnos-Dyrrhachion-Durrës* (Tirana, 2004)

Isaac, B., *The Limits of the Empire, The Roman Army in the East* (Oxford, 1992)

James, S.T., 'The Boston Helmet: a preliminary account of a Parthian-Roman Era artefact at the Museum of Fine Arts' in R. Collins & F. McIntosh, *Life in the Limes: Studies of the people and objects of the Roman frontiers* (Oxbow, 2014), 96–104

Kramer, V.S., 'Das Grabmonument der T. Flavius Mikkalus aus Perinth' in *Kolner Jarhrbuch* 27 (1994), 99–116

Mayer, F.G. & V. Karageorghis, *Paphos, History and Archaeology* (Nicosia, 1984)

Nicolle, D., *Rome's Enemies (5): The Desert Frontier*, MAA 243 (London, 1991)

Novichenkova, N.G., 'Roman military equipment from the sanctuary of the pass of Gurzufskoe Sedlo' in *WFI* (1998, No. 2), 51–56

Popescu, G.A. et al, *Traiano, ai confini dell'Impero, catalogo della mostra* (Rome, 1998)

Robinson, H.R., *The Armour of Imperial Rome* (London, 1975)

Russell, J., 'Cilicia – Nutrix Virorum: Cilicians abroad in peace and war during Hellenistic and Roman times' in *Anatolia Antiqua*, Tome 1 (1991), 283–297

Speidel, M.A., 'Connecting Cappadocia. The contribution of the Roman Imperial army' in V. Cojocaru, A. Coşkun & M. Dana, 'Interconnectivity in the Mediterranean and Pontic world during the Hellenistic and Roman periods' in *Pontica et Mediterranea*, Vol. III (Cluj-Napoca, 2014) 625–640

Stiebel, G.D., *Armis et litteris; the military equipment of early Roman Palestine in light of archaeological and historical sources* (PhD thesis, University College London, 2007)

PLATE COMMENTARIES

A: DACIA

A1: Legionary cavalryman, *vexillatio* of *Legio XIII Gemina*; Apulum (Alba Julia), second half of 2nd century AD

Reconstructed from a terracotta plaque, he has the new Heddernheim-type helmet (Robinson's Cavalry Sports Type G), with an eagle *protome*. The scale armour is of the new type fastened on the breast by a system employing two central embossed plaques. He has javelins (*verutta*) attached to his saddle.

A2: *Sagittarius, Cohors I Ituraeorum*; First Dacian War, c. AD 101

An archer of one of the many units of *sagittarii* employed for Trajan's wars wears a segmented 'spangenhelm'-type helmet of Sarmato-Danubian origin, and is protected by a leather *corium* as illustrated on Trajan's Column, together with others wearing scale and mail elements. The Ituraeans occupied an area north of Mt Hermon, centred on their capital at Chalcis; his footwear is Levantine in origin, and he carries a powerful composite bow.

A3: *Draconarius, Cohors II Aurelia Dacorum*; Porolissum, AD 166

Excavations at Kaloz in Hungary reveal that auxiliaries of Dacian origin fought with the Daco-Getican *falx* (here half-hidden, in his left hand) during Marcus Aurelius's Marcomannic wars along the Danube frontier. This standard-bearer's helmet is the splendid bronze specimen from Ostrov, and he carries a red-lacquered, dog-headed *balaur* or *draco*.

B: MOESIA SUPERIOR & INFERIOR

B1: *Miles gregarius, Legio I Italica*; Novae, 1st – 2nd century AD

This common soldier wears the bronze *lorica segmentata* of Corbridge A type, of which fragments from Novae point to stud-and-slot fastenings between the back upper plates (as also found in the Lucius Magus cuirass from Gamala in Palestine). His iron helmet of Imperial Gallic typology was recently found in Bulgaria (see page 46).

B2: *Eques* dressed for Hippika Gymnasia, *Legio XI Claudia Pia Fidelis*; Durostorum, AD 116

The spectacular equipment worn for the cavalry 'sports' – displays of military horsemanship – included beautiful masked helmets like that from Durostorum, decorated with sphinxes and garlands, and surmounted by the golden-yellow crest mentioned by Arrian. Note his linen cuirass reinforced with small scales, resembling a depiction of Alexander the Great, and the Scythian/Iranian costume, which we copy from the Mithraeum at Capua.

B3: *Centurio, Legio VII Claudia*; Viminacium, AD 88

This veteran centurion of Domitian's Dacian war displays a precious specimen of silvered Weisenau helmet, with a *crista transversa* of silver plumes. His armour and equipment are those typical of his rank: a cuirass of ridged scales, silvered iron greaves, and the *vitis* vinewood staff. His Pompeii-type sword, copied from a specimen from Dubravica, is concealed here by the captured Dacian embossed bronze shield.

C: MACEDONIA, EPIRUS & ACHAIA

C1: Crescens, *Eques Singularis Augusti*; Macedonia or Moesia Superior, 2nd century AD

The stele of the guardsman Crescens shows a small round shield attached to his saddle, and a number of javelins; he probably specialized in javelin-throwing, and was perhaps termed a *lanciarius* or *gaesatus*. He is wearing a *pectorarium*, over his *subarmalis* leather jerkin fitted with hanging *pteryges*, and his gilded and embossed helmet with a fronton is an actual specimen; the multicolored crest is from the Apollonia mosaic in modern Albania.

C2: *Stratiotas* of the Dyrrachium garrison; Epirus, 1st century BC – 1st century AD

This locally enlisted Illyrian soldier, copied from a partial figure sculpted on a limestone sarcophagus at Dyrrachium now in the Muzeu Arkeologjik, Durres, has a very Greek appearance. The pseudo-Attic decorated helmet conforms to local taste, and is visible in other sculptures of the period. The armour is a local variant of the *linothorax*, similar to those represented on the Julii Mausoleum (Glanum), and probably dates the original sculpture to the Augustan period. The embossed bronze shield is taken from local artworks representing trophies of weapons.

C3: Gaius Valerius Valens, *Legio VIII Augusta*; Corinth, Achaia, mid-1st century AD

This legionary, copied from his detailed funerary image, wears his fastened *paenula* marching cloak partly folded up over the shoulders, giving the characteristic 'W' shape at the front, and the hood folded round his neck. By simply flipping the 'tails' up onto his shoulders Valerius has easy access to his sidearms. From a belt hang five 'apron' straps, with up to five studs visible and lunate terminals with secondary pendants. Note that the apron is represented as passing under the *cingula* belts for his sword and dagger, and extends only half way down towards the hem of the *tunica*.

D: THRACIA, BITHYNIA & PONTUS

D1: Romano-Thracian *archon* of local auxiliaries; Anchialos, Thracia, end 1st century AD

The rich grave of a Thracian chieftain at Karaagatsch in modern Bulgaria has yielded a precious conical helmet, decorated with images of Apollo, Zeus, Athena, Ares, Nike

Terracotta plaque from Apulum, Dacia, second half of 2nd century AD, representing a cavalryman – see Plate A1. (Muzeul Nazional al Unirii, Alba Julia, inv. 9575 R; photo courtesy Dr Andrei Negin)

and Hermes. The only armour element found in the grave were the gilded scales forming the neck protection of the helmet. In other Thracian graves only spearheads were found; perhaps the owners went into battle protected only by leather or other organic corselets – but we cannot exclude the simplest explanation: that armour was owned, but not sacrificed by being included among the grave-goods.

D2: *Miles gregarius, Legio XIII Gemina*; Cyzicus, Bithynia, AD 197

This legionary of Severus's campaign against the Parthians is of Greco-Syrian origin, and wears the military costume that began to be widespread in the Roman army of the Severan period. The long-sleeved tunic (*paragauda*) is decorated with vertical silk *clavi* terminating in two *segmenta*. It is worn together with tight-fitting trousers of *anaxyrides* type, under a fringed *sagum* cloak. Note the *udones* (socks) worn inside hobnailed goatskin *calcei*. The ring-pommel *spatha* sword, from a Mesopotamian find, is already hung on his left side, from a baldric decorated with *phalerae* that passes through a bracket on the face of the scabbard.

D3: Bosphoran infantryman of Romano-Pontic garrison; Trabzon, Pontus, before AD 69

Copied from a gravestone from Panthicapea, this represents a Romano-Pontic infantryman of the Bosphorani. This Hellenistic type of helmet figures in at least two Roman-period archaeological finds in the Pontic and Bosphoran regions. The scale armour is Hellenistic in shape, but we reconstruct it from Roman bronze scales found in this area. The shield shows typical appliqué metallic lightning bolts. He is armed with a long Bosphoran spear and a *gladius* of Pompeii type, of which fragments have been found in the Chersonese region of Crimea.

E: ASIA, GALATIA & CYPRUS

E1: Markos Aurelios Diodoros; Hierapolis, Asia, second half of 2nd century AD

Markos was a *diogmitas* or paramilitary soldier employed on security duties; his stele shows him with his hunting-dog. The half-armour of banded leather is worn over a *subarmalis* showing a striped effect, suggesting a thick felt or padded garment anticipating the *vamvakion* and *aketon* of the Byzantine period. He is armed with a long spear and an

old-fashioned *machaira* curved, single-eged sword. Note his *cothurni* boots of Hellenic style.

E2: *Eques, Ala I Tracum Herculana*; Galatia, AD 94

The Thracian origin of this cavalryman is suggested by his mask-helmet, copied from a find in Asia Minor; Arrian (*Tact.* XXXIV, 4) describes the yellow crests of cavalry helmets as *xanthai* or 'bright blond'. The scale armour and the harness fittings are from the excavations at Gordion. The shield is copied from one engraved on the Thracian helmet from Anchialos, though its domed boss is invisible here.

E3: Second *centurio, Cohors I, Legio XV Apollinaris*; Paphos, Cyprus, AD 69

We know that a centurion of this unit accompanied Titus to the island at this date. The Eastern legions' equipment made abundant use of leather and other organic materials, such as felt and linen. This centurion's armour is reconstructed from the Tilurium reliefs, frescoes from Pompeii, and the monument to Favonius Facilis in Colchester. The silvered crest is inserted on the top of an embossed pseudo-Attic helmet with fronton, found in Israel (David Xavier Collection). The greaves (*ocreae*) and vine-staff are conventional symbols of his rank.

F: LYCIA-PAMPHILIA, CILICIA & CRETA

F1: *Eques, Cohors IIII Raetorum Equitata*; Side, Lycia-Pamphylia, AD 114

Carrying his pseudo-Attic helmet, this cavalryman of a unit originally raised in today's Switzerland or Austria is wearing a *galericulum*, the cap worn under a helmet to cushion its weight and to absorb the impact of blows. A stele from Side shows him clad only in a leather corselet with attached ranges of short *pteryges*, as on the Adamklisi reliefs. The round *parma* cavalry shield and the javelin are from depictions on sarcophagi. Note the horse's heavy Thracian curb bit.

F2: Mounted archer, *Cohors I Cretum Sagittariorum Equitata*; Gortyna, Creta, 1st – 2nd century AD

The sources list a large number of Eastern archer units which participated in the Dacian wars, such as *Cohors II Flavia Commagenorum Equitata Sagittariorum*, and *Cohors I Cretum Sagittariorum Equitata*. The reliefs on Trajan's Column help in the reconstruction of these famous bowmen, who served in the Roman army for centuries. He wears a segmented helmet made of 16 yellow-metal plates, over a felt

Unusually complete iron helmet of Weisenau typology, late 1st century AD, from the area of Philippopolis, Thracia – see Plate B1. It retains appliqué copper-alloy decorations, including the rosettes on the front of the bowl below the 'peak' brow-guard. The knob at the apex and the handle at the rear have parallels with a contemporary helmet from Aquincum (Budapest). (Private collection, National Archaeological Museum, Plovdiv; photos courtesy of the owner)

cap. His ringmail corselet has 'dagged' borders, as on the Column; both his powerful composite bow, and the long-bladed sidearm in a red-painted leather scabbard, are reconstructed from finds at Masada. Note the capped quiver, and the strap-on spurs.

F3: *Stationarius*; Artanada, Cilicia, AD 101
This Isaurian mountaineer from south-central Anatolia, copied from the Adamkalayar rock reliefs, is a locally recruited policeman-cum-frontier guard. His tunic is confined by a knotted sash as a symbol of his military status. As well as his heavy *akontion* javelin he has a sidearm of *parazonium* type, worn in a copper-alloy scabbard from a baldric; this represents a variation from the standard *gladii hispanienses* usually visible on the rock reliefs. He is wearing a wild animal's pelt as a mantle, and Greek-style *cothurni* boots.

G: SYRIA, JUDAEA & CAPPADOCIA
G1: *Miles gregarius, Legio X Fretensis*; Jerusalem, Judaea, AD 70
This soldier (of the legion named 'From the Sicilian Strait', *fretum siculum*) is wearing a local tunic under his armour, and is based on finds made in Palestine. His Imperial Gallic helmet, made in yellow metal, has a broad horizontal neck-guard. His *lorica segmentata* has a fastening system for the overlapping back plates based on rivets sliding in slots, and riveted tie-loops for fastening the girdle plates. His *gladius* of Pompeii type has a scabbard faced with red leather, copper-alloy fittings, and copper-alloy attachments to a leather belt fitted with silver-plated mounts. His rectangular, red-painted *scutum* shows the blazon of his legion; finds in Palestine suggest that the bonded-on leather facing was not merely decorative but was integral to the construction of the shield. Note the *falx muralis*, a socketed, leaf-shaped spear with a sickle-like extension for use in siege warfare. Its employment at the siege of Jotapata is described by Josephus (*BJ*, III, 225), and a specimen was found at Gamala. At his feet are reconstructions of a *manica* from Masada, and the Coolus-Hagenau helmet from Gamala.

G2: Roman cavalry commander; Syria, 2nd century AD
He is reconstructed with the open helmet from the rich finds in the Nawa grave. He is armed with a long sword (blade 71cm/28ins); a spear or fighting javelin (head 11cm/4.3ins long); and two daggers. The bronze scales of the cuirass had a maximum length of 4cm, with metal wire reciprocal fastenings and attached to the backing with large nails. The excavation report speaks of shoulder-guards, now disappeared. Unusually in Roman archaeology, the decorative pieces of the *cymation* at the waist were preserved. Behind him, note a combined bowcase/quiver.

G3: *Miles gregarius, Legio XII Fulminata*; Melitene, Cappadocia, second half of 1st century AD
This soldier of the 'Lightning-bolts Legion' is copied from a monument of the Flavian period (today in the Villa Torlonia, Rome), commemorating the Jewish War. The leather *corium* is characterized by the presence of shoulder-guards. Note the *cingulum bullatum*, and the highly decorated pseudo-Attic helmet.

H: AEGYPTUS, ARABIA & CYRENAICA
H1: City guard, Aegyptus, c. AD 130
This figure from the Hadrianic period is based on the famous linen shroud in the Pushkin Museum, Moscow. The yellow-brown colour in the source suggests banded leather body armour, similar to those illustrated on Anatolian monuments. He is armed with a *lancea*, and his head is slightly protected by a leather cap, whose shape in the original painting recalls an actual later specimen from Dura Europos.

H2: *Eques, Cohors II Hispanorum Scutata Cyrenaica Equitata*; Cyrene, late 1st century AD
This part-mounted unit fought in the Dacian wars. The cavalryman, copied mainly from Trajan's Column, is protected by a simple leather *corium*, and by a pseudo-Attic helmet which seems the type most often represented on monuments in Cyrenaica even before the reign of Severus. The internal reinforcement of his shield corresponds with original specimens from Vindonissa. He wears cavalry *caligae*, with strap-on spurs and triangular hobnails.

H3: *Eques, Cohors III Ulpia Petraeorum Milliaria Equitata Sagittaria*; Arabia, AD 107
Arab archers were recorded in Roman service by Josephus (*BJ*, III, 168, 211, 262) as early as the reign of Vespasian. This horse-archer, from a double-size part-mounted unit raised by Trajan, is based partly on the tombstone of Maris Casitilius of a different Arab unit, who seems to wear a 'sports' helmet similar to the Qidron Valley or Jordan specimen. Levantine arrows were constructed with a wooden fore-end fixed to a long reed shaft. Note the lamellar armour, worn over Parthian-style dress.

Depiction of a soldier of *Legio XIII Gemina* bringing in a prisoner, on a relief from Nicomedia in Bithynia commemorating the campaign of AD 197 against the Parthians – see Plate D2. This and other sculptures from the province show typical Severan-period costume innovations such as sleeved tunics and long trousers, here worn beneath a *sagum* cloak. (Archaeological Museum, Izmit; author's photo, courtesy of the Museum)

INDEX

Figures in **bold** *refer to images and captions.*